Using New Web Tools in the Primary Classroom

How can we ensure we use technology effectively with young children?

Using New Web Tools in the Primary Classroom is for all teachers interested in the application of new web-based ICTs to primary teaching. It offers a justification for using Web 2.0 tools and explores tangible ways in which technologies such as blogs, wikis, podcasting, media sharing and social networking sites can enhance classroom practice, teaching and learning.

Considering key issues such as how children learn, curriculum, policy, and children's prior experiences of ICT, this book focuses on the expectations and needs of the child and how technology can be unlocked to meet those needs now and in the future. Key ideas considered include:

- diverse views of social software in education
- using web tools to create and reinforce stimulating learning environments
- teacher skills and the availability of suitable technology
- competing demands of government policies and curriculum
- practical ideas for enriching learning through social software: children as producers of knowledge, as explorers, and as communicators.

Enhanced with reflective questions and tasks to support your own thinking, and with practical ideas for using web-based ICTs in a range of subjects and in topic work, *Using New Web Tools in the Primary Classroom* is a rich resource for all student and practising primary school teachers. Those on Education Studies courses interested in new internet technologies and their potential to enhance learning within primary schools will also find much food for thought.

David Barber is Lecturer in E-Learning at Bishop Grosseteste University College, UK

Linda Cooper is a Senior Lecturer at Chichester University, UK

Using New Web Tools in the Primary Classroom

A practical guide for enhancing teaching
and learning

David Barber and Linda Cooper

Routledge
Taylor & Francis Group

LONDON AND NEW YORK

First published 2012
by Routledge
2 Park Square, Milton Park, Abingdon, Oxon OX14 4RN

Simultaneously published in the USA and Canada
by Routledge
711 Third Avenue, New York, NY 10017

Routledge is an imprint of the Taylor & Francis Group, an informa business

British Library Cataloguing in Publication Data
A catalogue record for this book is available from the British Library

Library of Congress Cataloging in Publication Data
Cooper, Linda.
Using new Web tools in the primary classroom : a practical guide for enhancing teaching and learning / Linda Cooper & David Barber.
p. cm.
Includes bibliographical references and index.
1. Teaching--Great Britain--Computer network resources. 2. Education--Great Britain--Computer network resources. 3. Internet in education--Great Britain. 4. Teaching--Great Britain--Aids and devices. 5. Education, Primary--Curricula--Great Britain. 6. Primary school teaching--Great Britain. I. Barber, David. II. Title.
LB1044.87.C675 2012
371.33'44678--dc23
2011021201

ISBN: 978-0-415-59105-8 (hbk)
ISBN: 978-0-415-59104-1 (pbk)
ISBN: 978-0-203-58474-3 (ebk)

Typeset in Times New Roman
by Taylor & Francis books

MIX
Paper from
responsible sources
FSC
www.fsc.org   FSC® C004839

Printed and bound in Great Britain by
TJ International Ltd, Padstow, Cornwall

Contents

List of Figures and Tables

Tables

Figures

Preface

Reading this book

This book is designed to be read by anyone who is interested in the application of new web-based ICTs to primary teaching. It is particularly relevant to anyone who works in the primary classroom or who is training to do so. In fact, the book has been designed with all these audiences in mind.

Using this book

This book can be read from cover to cover. It is divided into two sections, but a continuous theme is developed throughout. A detailed summary of the content is provided in the Introduction, but by way of very brief overview: the first section develops a justification for the use of Web 2.0 tools and thereby lays the ground-work for the second section, which contains a discussion of the specific and tangible ways in which these technologies can enhance classroom practice.

For those readers who are involved in initial teacher training or are reading this book as a means to developing skills in this area of teaching practice, most chapters in the first section contain reflective and practical tasks. These are designed to either back up the ideas developed in the text or to support the development of confidence and skills in relevant areas. In the same spirit, the second section combines descriptions of classroom activities with clearly demarcated sections that focus on practical considerations relating to the web tools involved. These are designed to provide practical assistance to any reader who hopes to use these ideas or to build upon them in their own practice.

A note on commonly used terms

A concerted effort has been made to avoid technical terminology and where it is impossible to do so specialist terms are explained carefully within the text. However, there is one area of terminology that requires comment at this stage. The introduction spends some time examining the language of Web 2.0. We look at some of the problems with this term and come to a definition which allows us to use it as a general label for the technologies discussed in subsequent chapters. However, we also use this discussion as an opportunity to introduce some related terms that couch the general phenomenon of Web 2.0 in more meaningful language. The reader who dips into sections of this book, or who reads chapters out of order should understand that terms like 'social software' and 'social media' and 'Web 2.0' are used synonymously.

Section 1

Understanding web tools in the primary classroom

Introduction

In this book we argue that there is an urgent need to rethink some emerging web technologies for use in the primary school classroom. We intend to demonstrate that there are compelling reasons for embedding the use of these tools within processes of learning and teaching, but before we start to expand on this theme, we need to answer one fundamental issue: what are these 'new web tools'?

For many people the World Wide Web and the internet are synonymous. The terms are often used interchangeably because it was the creation of the World Wide Web in the very early 1990s that made the technical infrastructure of the internet accessible to the majority of people. The internet had been around for almost 30 years before this point, but it was not until the development of what we now refer to simply as 'the web' that this technology started to make dramatic impacts on our lifestyles (Naughton 1999).

The web itself is founded on innovations like hypertext – the concept of creating 'clickable' links that are embedded into the content of a page and allow navigation between documents – and web browsers – simple software applications that display web documents and manage our navigation as we move between them. These are still the fundamental building blocks of modern internet use; few of us could recall or even imagine an internet without them. Nevertheless, the World Wide Web and the ways in which we interact with it have changed radically over the last 20 or so years.

The most obvious of these changes is seen in activities like social networking, blogging, media sharing and the creation of large scale collaborative undertakings like wikis; activities that involve ordinary users in the process of content creation. In the early years of the World Wide Web, these kinds of activities were relatively limited. Creating web content required considerable expertise and some cost to the contributor. Today, much more of the content that people encounter on the web has been created by ordinary users in the course of their day to day activities. Importantly, they have been able to do this with the kinds of skills acquired through basic word processing and e-mail communication and at no personal expense.

This has inspired the creation of terms like the 'participatory web' or the 'read/write web' or, most commonly 'Web 2.0' (O'Reilly 2005). Such terms are often criticised because they create the impression that the web has somehow changed. This is misleading, but the World Wide Web *does* look and feel different now to how it looked and felt ten years ago. The technologies that underpinned this explosion in user generated content have been around for almost as long as the web itself. Mark Zuckerberg's initial versions of what we now know as Facebook were based on a well established kind of web tool that invited users to compare and rank pairs of photographs. Flickr, a popular photo-sharing website, was originally part of an online gaming site known as a Massive Multiplayer Online Game (MMOG), which derived from a form of online entertainment known as MUDs (Multi User Dungeons) and therefore predated the invention of the web itself.

However, the development of these technologies into the creation of easy to use tools was relatively recent. In both the cases outlined above, the reworking of old technologies led to a phenomenon that was never anticipated by the original creators. Zuckerberg watched from his college dormitory as his 'Facebook' spread virally, first through his college and ultimately around the world. The owners of Flickr ended up shelving their game site and focused on the much more popular photo-sharing service instead. In each case the development of services that gave users control over the content and presentation of web pages appeared to tap into a strongly felt and previously unsatisfied need, to be able to express oneself in an online environment.

In this book we are interested in the tools that underpin services like Facebook and YouTube and Flickr, tools that can be accessed independently on the web or via school based internet services like Virtual Learning Environments. All of them allow users to create and share content in a social environment and so are referred to here as social software. However, let us be clear, what are these new tools that we are talking about and what do they actually allow us to do?

Blogs

The weblog or blog exemplifies the problem in trying to identify neat boundaries between the so-called Web 2.0 and its antecedents. It is almost impossible to identify the first blog as the form emerged gradually (Rosenburg 2009: 81), but it is certain that the origins of the genre belonged in the era of the web's first generation. Resembling a diary or journal, a blog is normally a chronologically organised sequence of entries composed of text, images, video and even interactive content like games or quizzes. Blogs can either occupy their own dedicated space on the web, with their own web address, or appear as part of another type of site, like a social networking page. Specialist sites offer aspiring bloggers personal pages and provide simple tools known as 'WYSIWYG' (What You See Is What You Get) editors, that allow authors to compose entries using tools that are familiar to most people from basic word processing applications. When instructed the editor then translates finished content on to the webpage automatically, rendering the process straightforward and attractively un-technical.

Many blogs take the form of a personal journal, recording aspects of an individual's day to day experience. They have sprung up around virtually every aspect of personal and professional life, but the blog is not private – like a diary – or a place for introspective reflection – like many forms of journal. In addition to this the blog is also characterised by hypertext, 'links', in other words, that connect them to other blogs or other pages on the web. Although they cover a wide variety of subjects, therefore, most blogs have a preoccupation with web-content within their chosen field. The blog is not just a way in which web content is created, therefore, but an important medium in which that content is analysed and evaluated.

Wikis

The term 'wiki' was introduced by Ward Cunningham, who is credited with creating the first example of this form of website. It refers to the 'wiki' or 'quick' bus that connects the terminals in Honolulu's airport. Ward Cunningham chose the name as his aim in installing the 'wikiwikiWeb' in 1995 was to create a publically accessible database that could be updated quickly by a large community of online users (Ward Cunningham and Leuf 2005). The contributor to a wiki uses a simple WYSIWYG editor, which they access by clicking a button on the page itself, to generate new pages or edit existing ones within the wiki site. In addition to this, hyperlinks are used very heavily to connect pages into an interlinking resource, just like they do in blogs. In this manner they draw on the power of the web to connect people, but the emphasis in wikis falls on active and direct collaboration between members of the online community.

A good example of how this happens is provided by the world of Massive Multiplayer Online Games. These games attract large groups of players to a game environment that is characterised by uncertainty. It is governed by rules, like the laws of physics in the 'real' world, which are not immediately apparent and can only be understood and exploited by careful observation and complex calculation. The game designers generally provide the minimum of information, requiring players to figure the mechanics of the game environment out for themselves. Given this situation, one of the common responses of the game-playing community is to create a wiki where individuals can contribute the outcomes of their own experience in the game environment for the benefit of all. Someone creates the wiki and then all players can access and develop the site adding new pages as they see fit or editing and commenting on the content created by other people.

Wikis do more than allow people to make web content, therefore. They are places where people with a common purpose can come together and work collaboratively; not just in the gathering information but in the construction of knowledge. As we shall see, wikis have their detractors. You don't need to demonstrate any particular qualifications or experience to contribute to a wiki and are effectively anonymous. This stands in stark contrast to traditional approaches to knowledge creation that privilege specialists with status and reputations to maintain. However, the modern reality is that the web has made information much more readily available than it ever was before and its release is much less strictly governed and controlled. This means that we are obliged to discriminate in our use of information and wikis are one of the forums in which this mass of digital content can be discussed and exposed to critical scrutiny.

Podcasting and media sharing

A Podcast is a multimedia recording that can be distributed via the internet. The word podcast is derived from the acronym 'POD', which stands for Playable On Demand (Hammersley 2004), and the suffix 'cast' which recalls more traditional forms of media distribution like broadcasting. It therefore conveys the sense that the podcast is a form of media that is designed to be consumed by the viewer at a time and from a place that suits them, not according to a preset schedule like conventional media offerings encountered on television.

Most podcasts are reasonably short in length and often accompany other media or real-world events. Many popular television and radio programmes have podcasts associated with them, for example, and podcasts can be used to give interested parties insights into processes or activities that they would not normally be able to access. However, perhaps the most interesting possibility provided by the podcast is the potential for ordinary people to produce multimedia resources of a kind that was normally open only to broadcast companies and which would require significant technical expertise and official permission to distribute by conventional means. The podcast can be created using simple sound or video recording equipment and can be distributed using freely available software and services accessed on the internet.

A related form of tool is found in the media sharing sites like Flickr and YouTube, which allow users to upload, share and browse photographs and videos respectively. Unlike podcasts these sites host material that is intended to be viewed on the site itself, which has two major effects. First the author of the material enjoys a higher profile and a more interactive relationship with his or her audience through a comment function that invites feedback from viewers. Second, consumers of the material are also able to browse very large volumes of user generated content creating a potentially rich and exciting experience.

Social networking sites

The social networking site is, as the name suggests, a web based service that provides a platform for the development of social networks. There are very many different social networking services, which typically provide a facility for creating a personal profile and support communication with an effectively limitless number of online contacts. The differences between various social networking services typically arise in relation to the tools that the user employs to communicate with contacts, to develop their personal profile and to pass time recreationally with other members of an online network.

These differences can have a very profound effect on the character of the site and the ways in which the social network operates. Sites like Facebook, which incorporate numerous games and dynamic communication tools like the 'wall' – a space where contacts can leave comments – suit those looking for a personal social hub that they can check and update on a regular basis. MySpace, on the other hand, with the prominence it gives to video content and songs, is popular among those who want to base their network around musical tastes. Increasingly, different social networking sites are diverging in order to suit people of specific age groups, geographical origin and personal or professional preoccupations.

Social bookmarking sites and Really Simple Syndication (RSS)

Bookmarking refers to the processes of identifying useful or interesting websites and creating lists of hyperlinks that provide easy access to them. Many people already maintain lists of 'favourites' with tools provided by their web-browsers. This provides a quick and simple means of accessing frequently used web-pages, but these lists are stored on the PC you are using at the time and cannot be accessed from elsewhere. An advantage of using social bookmarking sites like Delicious or Diigo is that the bookmarks you create are stored on a publicly accessible website and are consequentially available from any computer that can connect to the internet. However, this approach has another much more significant result; it allows you to share your lists and to search or browse the bookmarks of other users – hence the term *social* bookmarking.

Also known as Rich Site Summary, RSS is a means of automating the process of importing content from one site to another. Normally used with blogs, by people who want to follow multiple authors without having to trawl between multiple sites, RSS can be thought of as a means of subscribing to content on the web. To start your subscription you simply paste a URL (web-address) that is provided by the website owner into your 'aggregator', which becomes, through the application of several feeds, a dynamic mosaic of your favourite web-content. The content is updated automatically, so you are likely to find new stuff every time you login, thereby saving you the time consuming and often uncertain process of visiting multiple websites. Of course there is no reason why networks of people cannot share a single aggregator and, used in conjunction with social book-marking tools, this facility allows groups of learners to create windows on the web that open on specified sources of content that can be evaluated and assessed in a critical way.

And many, many more

These then, are the applications that are most commonly associated with Web 2.0. It is important to understand that they are really underpinned by similar principles and similar technologies. The social networking site, for example, shares characteristics with media sharing sites and blogs, while blogs and wikis both depend on very similar content creation tools. However, a complete survey of Web 2.0 tools would be nigh on impossible as they are extremely numerous and very varied. The principles encountered in the preceding survey can be put to countless purposes and the underlying tools are combined in all sorts of ways in order to support specific activities or to create a particular type of environment.

Take Flickr for example, a photo-sharing site that allows users to upload photographs, annotate them and share their 'albums' with other visitors. It is a media sharing site, but also shares characteristics with blogs and with social networking sites and therefore exemplifies the ways in which Web 2.0 services merge and overlap with one another. However, the experience of using Flickr derives from the very specific combination of tools that it provides. These allow visitors to not only search for photographs with specific content, but also embed all the content in the world map provided by Google, providing a stimulating and exciting way of sharing and discovering images. In later chapters we will come across many of these sites, but it is important to acknowledge – even at this early stage – that to try and comprehend today's World Wide Web is to try and keep up with an exciting, but ever changing mosaic of different activities and services.

Having defined some of the key tools addressed in this book under the heading of 'social software', we can now return to that statement encountered at the very beginning of this introduction. What do we mean by rethinking these tools? Why do we think there is such an urgent need to embed social software into processes of learning and teaching? And what are the 'issues' that we alluded to before? Of course these are questions that will preoccupy us for much of what comes in later chapters, but it is useful to outline the discussion here and to anticipate some of the major themes.

The word 'rethinking' has been used deliberately, for many of us have preconceptions about tools like blogs and media sharing sites that derive from our own encounters with them or from more general ideas about the role of ICT in schools. If one looks at the ways in which the tools outlined above are used online, one can get a rather jaundiced impression of their usefulness in education. Levels of participation in social software are often much lower and more sporadic than grand terms like 'the participatory web' imply. What is more, the output that one does encounter on the open web is not always of the quality, tone or presentational standard that we would like to see in class.

Take media sharing as an example. A survey of websites like YouTube provides abundant evidence for the ways in which Web 2.0 tools are used and misused. This provides plenty of ammunition to those who argue that ICTs and the internet encourage antisocial and even selfdestructive behaviour. It is just as easy to point to the short-comings of sites like Wikipedia or to the thousands of abandoned blogs. Many of the opinions expressed in these forums seem credulous and poorly informed and are char-acterised by the uncritical reproduction of outlandish opinions and, sometimes, even the verbatim reproduction of material from unverified sources.

All of this makes the internet seem a very inappropriate and even dangerous place for learning to take place. However, to dismiss the tools on the basis of this kind of evidence is to entirely miss their potential. For one thing, negative views are very easily overstated. Communication on the web is often very positive and constructive. Pointless and vulgar criticism is normally balanced or at least challenged by positive remarks. Offensive and deliberately provocative contributions are normally censured by others in the community. For another, most of the websites and services mentioned so far are first and foremost recreational spaces. We should not, therefore, confuse the tool with the content that it produces, particularly when that content was produced by communities and for purposes that are very different from those encountered in education.

Rethinking, therefore, refers to a process of disentangling the tools and their potential from the content they produce on the open web. It requires us to understand the ways in which this content distorts our view of social software and to identify the essential attributes of the tools so that we can evaluate their educational potential objectively. This is the subject of the first chapter, which explores these issues in greater depth and leads to a working definition of the key tools that is appropriate for an educational application.

This leads naturally to a consideration of the second question: why the urgency? It has to be acknowledged that there is a substantial body of educational theory that opposes the notion that ICT should be given a greater role to play in primary education. Influential trends within schooling, such as those following Steiner's spiritualistic view of education (SWSF 2010: FAQ) or Montessori's emphasis on sensory development (Montessori 1917 [1965]: 128) have developed a hostile attitude to the use of computers by young children.

Commentators of recent years like Palmer have been critical of the role of ICT in the lives of young people and have presented it as a contributor to 'toxic' childhood (Palmer 2006). In many cases their criticisms rest on valid concerns, or at least raise spectres that are worthy of serious consideration. However, many of these opinions do not actually appear to refer to the tools themselves but to patterns of behaviour that are observed in non-educational contexts or are associated with poorly devised educa-tional uses. In any case there are much more positive commentaries too and the second chapter explores the diverse views of social software in education.

The third chapter argues that it is possible to construct a rationale for the use of social software based on three principles. The first derives from a consideration of the expectations of the child, the second from their future needs and the third from the pedagogical potential of the tools themselves. Put briefly it is argued that children come to formal education with certain expectations of learning that are increasingly formed by their use of the internet. This is not simply a question of indulging habits or patterns of behaviour that children may bring to school from outside. It involves seriously engaging with the question of how formal education relates to broader learning processes that are located in many situations and increasingly reflect the influence of the internet as an information space.

Second, the primary school children of today are going to need sophisticated critical and analytical skills appropriate to a world that is becoming more and more dependent on the Web. While we may still bemoan the perceived inadequacies of the internet as an information space, the fault lies not with the dumb, un-inquisitive technical infrastructure of the internet, but with the information skills of the people who use it. It is therefore imperative to cultivate a level of information fluency that will make the primary school children of today the discriminating producers and consumers of knowledge of the future, an aim that can only ever hope to be achieved if we engage them at an early stage in activities that use the internet as a learning environment.

Third, it is argued that there are tangible pedagogical reasons for engaging with the Web 2.0 tools outlined above. In contradiction to the arguments put forward by many sceptics it is proposed here that tools like blogs and wikis allow teachers to create stimulating learning opportunities that do not undermine the importance of communication and collaboration in the construction of knowledge, but positively emphasise and reinforce it. Such tools, used well, allow us to couch learning in creative, problem based situations that engage children in authentic activities that align well with the key objectives of the primary curriculum.

In the fourth chapter we turn to some of the issues faced by teachers in deploying these tools within that curriculum. These cover a range of different areas including teacher skills, the availability of suitable technology and the competing demands of government policies and the curriculum. However, in addition to these there is a larger and in many ways more urgent issue that forms the heart of this section of the book. This concerns the wider impact of the internet, not just upon the wider society within which children are growing and learning, but within the minds of the children themselves. It therefore picks up some themes from the third chapter, but goes much further in developing discussion around notions of the personalisation of learning.

This then brings us to the second section of the book, which sets out to provide trainees, NQTs and experienced teachers alike with inspiration and support in their use of social software. This section brings research, case studies and working examples of reproducible classroom activities together in a discussion of how social software can be used in primary education. It contains three main sections which examine a range of Web 2.0 tools from a number of different curriculum perspectives. Each section takes its title from roles that social software helps children to inhabit in relation to their learning. They explore how children can be supported in their emergence as 'creators and producers', 'explorers' and 'communicators'. If Section 1 is about understanding social software then Section 2 addresses the question of using social software and doing so in a constructive and effective fashion.

Chapter 1

Rethinking social software for the primary classroom

This chapter aims to identify the characteristics of specific social software tools that make them appropriate for the primary classroom.

It explores the underlying characteristics that establish the relevance of the following tools:

- social networking sites;
- blogs;
- wikis;
- podcasts and media sharing sites;
- RSS aggregators and social bookmarking services.

As the term social software implies, many of these tools are defined by the opportunities that they create for interaction between users. Most of them are effectively communication or collaboration tools and are specifically designed in order to enhance cooperation and to manage coordinated activity within a community of learners. In doing so, most provide new, sociable ways of exploring and representing knowledge and provide new opportunities for creative expression. As such, we might expect them to support a satisfying learning experience that is authentic, in the sense that a wider audience can always be assumed, and which therefore requires the learner to become more responsible and more independent in their thinking (Gokhale 1995).

From its conception the internet was designed as a communication network and familiar tools like e-mail can be traced to the very earliest days of its development. The very first traffic on the internet was sent on the 15th of October 1969 and within two years, at a time when there were only 15 computers on the network, e-mail came into being. In 1972 a means for logging on to remote computers and exchanging files was introduced. It was called 'Request For Comment' (RFC), and from this time the notion of a network and of an 'inter-net' community was established.

By the late 1980s, as the computer and telecommunications equipment required for joining the web become more accessible, trends emerged that made the internet more open to non technical audiences. A means of navigating networks via menus was eventually overtaken by the now familiar system of 'hypertext', where links between pages were embedded into readable blocks of text, and with the development of the first internet browser what we now recognise as the World Wide Web was born.

Since then communication across the web has exploded and the increasing availability of web tools that allow ordinary web users to create content has coincided with an extraordinary increase in internet use. Of course a range of factors might have played a part in this. The increasing speed and reliability of internet connections combined with falling subscription costs must have played a role, as well as the development of technologies that allow people to communicate across the web from handheld devices and mobile phones. However, as suggested in the introduction, the opportunities for increased participation, communication and creative expression can also be seen to have played a part.

In this chapter we shall look at some of the tools that stand at the vanguard of this movement towards increased participation. This will involve returning to some of the themes identified in the introduction, but we shall now seek to define them in a way that makes it possible to envisage a role in education, illustrating the process of rethinking that was previously alluded to in more detail.

Social networking

Representative of the newer and more sophisticated tools are social networking sites, which have made it easier than ever before for people to maintain and extend social networks within an online environment. These tools have their antecedents in older web technologies; sites like Geocities had previously offered people the opportunity to create 'homepages' where they could develop an online profile. However, sites like Facebook and MySpace triggered a massive increase in this kind of activity.

In trying to explain this phenomenon we might look at the nature of the tools themselves, which had become easier to access and allowed people with little expertise to create satisfying results. At the same time, improvements in the infrastructure underpinning internet use – faster internet connections for example – allowed users to use and exchange media like photographs, music and videos more easily, improving the overall experience. However, it is also almost certainly the case that the network generated its own momentum. As more people joined, participation looked more attractive and being part of the network became a significant and meaningful act. Put another way, social networking is not just the expression of a pre-existing need, but a phenomenon in its own right and the possibility exists, one that has variously interested, excited and confounded educators, that this phenomenon might be tapped for educational purposes.

As with so many web tools it is tempting to try and define social networking sites by reference to the content they have created. When looking at them closely, one finds personal information, photographs, music, comments from 'friends' or visitors, links to other people's networking sites or to websites outside the network, feeds from other networking tools like Twitter and gadgets that support gaming or other recreational pastimes. What immediately incites interest is the volume of this information and how dynamic and how up to date it is. What tends to excite is the obvious enthusiasm that members – our own students and pupils among them – show for communication and interaction in what is ultimately a literate environment. What confounds is the difficulty in seeing an opening for educational activity in such a personal and firmly recreational space.

Of course there are obvious problems with promoting social networking within a primary education environment. A site that encourages children to share photographs with strangers or to create networks of social contacts based on the exchange of personal information could introduce obvious dangers: to the child, to the teacher and to the school. What is more, those social networks that do cater for children of the relevant age are deliberately maintained as adult free zones and place games at the heart of an interactive environment that is based on strictly regulated processes of social exchange. In Club Penguin, for example, children take a penguin as an in-game avatar that they can clothe and accessorise using 'coins' that they earn by playing mini-games. They can then meet and chat, in strictly monitored and limited ways, with the penguins of other children.

Nevertheless, there are reasons for educators to be interested in these sites and the activities that take place there. Sites like Club Penguin, Neo Pet and Moshimonsters are places where children can be seen to engage with social software and other users in complex interactions and processes of problem solving and enquiry. They learn how to control online environments that would baffle many adults and learn approaches to communicating and sharing information that they will employ in many other online situations in later life. Significantly they do so in a highly literate environment and acquire a view of the internet that emphasises its social characteristics. In this way the use of social networking sites by young children accords with Buckingham's argument that teaching with digital media can only follow from learning *about* them (Buckingham 2007: 74). What is more, in this context children are learning about digital media in an environment that reveals 'the emotional dimensions of our uses and interpretations of these media. ... that exceed mere "information"' (Buckingham 2007: 77).

The problem is how to translate this activity into a classroom scenario. One could envisage a social networking space in which this apparently compelling pattern of social interaction was attached to the attainment of learning goals, rather than achievements within gaming scenarios. There are examples of software packages that have been designed by or on behalf of schools, some of which have been tested and implemented and have started to generate interesting results. However, the problems associated with a social network that is designed for education and governed by teachers and by schools are significant.

For one thing, substantial financial investment and creative input would need to go into the creation and development of an environment that was as stimulating and engaging as the commercial equivalents. Interesting projects have created results, some even creating virtual worlds (Merchant 2007), but are significant undertakings. For another, the nature of the network is itself an important factor. On commercial social networking sites children can elect to socialise with their friends online, and are able to select who joins their network. At the same time, if they elect to meet 'new' people they are at liberty to do so anonymously and with people whose true identity is similarly ambiguous. Both these characteristics are potentially problematic. They are not necessarily suited to the needs of a fixed, classroom-based community of learners where the emphasis lies on inclusion and personalisation. However, remove this facility and it is uncertain how much of the appeal is lost in the process.

Nevertheless, we are entitled to ask whether we really need to adopt the version of social networking that we find on commercial networking sites into the classroom. Is it really sensible to try and translate 'social' networking – where social seems to equate to recreational – into an educational environment, or would it make more sense to look instead at the more fundamental aspects of the social networking phenomenon that we are interested in and the characteristics that support it?

As we suggested before, the main feature of social networking sites that attracts educators is their success in engaging users in communication and in the exchange of information within an online environment. Underpinning this success appears to be the sense of ownership and enthusiasm that the ability to publish a profile conveys; not just an online presence, but a self-portrayal that is independent of one's 'real' identity and gives all the opportunities for anonymity and play that this affords (Livingston 2008).

This is a good example of how social software can be assessed independently of the content it produces or of the context that its normal service environment imposes. Separated from the worryingly ungovernable network associated with the Facebook community, or from the deliberately frivolous nature of many child-friendly networking sites, we are left with the simpler but still intriguing phenomenon that we can apply in an educational context. Social networking can be reduced to the relatively simple notion of allowing pupils to create, refine and share online identities in the course of web-based activities. What might this achieve? Well quite simply, if we can hope to translate anything from the social networking environment we might hope to instil in children the same sense of ownership and commitment to the online activities that they engage with in classroom situations.

Logistical problems remain. The use of many social networking sites is either prohibited, due to age restrictions, or limited, due to the nature of the social networking site itself. For example, the educational potential of sites like Moshimonsters have been recognised and are featured on Teachers' TV (2008). However, the fact that some children are able to access an enhanced service through subscription payments presents issues relating to what is referred to as the digital divide: the impact of variations in parental income and understanding of the benefits of digital literacy on children's access to technology at home. This is a theme that is discussed in later chapters, but it is an example of the way in which commercial services can prove difficult to integrate into a learning context.

However, having identified the fundamental benefits of social networking for education, it is possible to start thinking about how to incorporate them into the learning environment independently of the commercial networks themselves. The ability to create virtual spaces in which identity can be expressed in a playful and creative way can be reproduced in a virtual learning environment, for example. We return to this theme later on, where we see that the principles of social networking can be applied to structured educational outcomes and promote opportunities for greater personalisation.

Blogging

Perhaps the most logical type of web tool to move to next is the weblog. If the social networking site supports the greatest amount of user activity it is the blog that has generated the largest volume of text. As we have seen the blog is a form of online journal that can be created by an individual or a group and maintained in the form of a series of time stamped entries. These entries can contain text, hyperlinks, images and – increasingly – multimedia content as well. They appear one after the other on a dedicated page that normally invites readers to subscribe via a 'feed' (see below) and provide access to personal information about the author, archives and web-links. Blogs become the focus for people with shared recreational, lifestyle or professional interests and can range in focus across virtually any topic you might imagine.

As a genre or phenomenon blogging has received a lot of bad press. Blogs are a mouthpiece for anyone who chooses to start one, regardless of how well informed, interesting or articulate they are. It is calculated that more than 50 blogs are started every minute (Blogpulse 2011) and it is probably safe to say that the vast majority are read by a very small audience or none whatsoever. If viewed from the perspective of someone accustomed to reading the work of professional journalists or peer reviewed scholarship, many examples of this form of writing look very poor indeed. Among those blogs that do take off, a sizeable number serve as a space where people with minority opinions and beliefs can find each other and celebrate a shared identity that is largely invisible in the embodied world. Worryingly, therefore, blogs can and do provide rallying points and safe spaces for the expression of antisocial, misanthropic and plain objectionable opinions.

This is all largely due to the architecture of the internet, which means that information can be exchanged anonymously, without scrutiny or censorship, and the ease with which almost everyone can access and master the blogging tools. However, these very same attributes create great potential as well. For members of dispersed religious or cultural diaspora or devotees of unusual pastimes, the range and scope of the internet – its ability to connect people across space, time zones and political boundaries – is a tremendous benefit. In other situations the anonymity afforded by the internet allows groups to form completely independently of cultural, ethnic or gender markers that define and constrain individuals within embodied communities. This is personally liberating and creates an environment for less inhibited creative and intellectual expression.

Many blogs command a sizeable readership and provide their authors with a useful profile within their chosen professional or social circle. They are a mechanism for extending one's network of professional associates and a mechanism for the sharing and comparing of ideas. This is largely supported by the comment function, which allows readers to respond to the blogger's posts. This also defines the blog as something distinct from a diary or personal journal as the blog is written with an audience in mind and is a dynamic environment in which ideas can be submitted and discussed. Unlike paper-based personal journals, blogs are also interconnected. They can be linked at a blog to blog level, where the author of one blog creates a link from her blog page to the blog page of another blogger in her circle, or at the level of the 'permalink' where a durable link is created between individual posts within two blogs (durable in the sense that the link continues to work over time, even if the target post is archived). This means that the notion of wider audience not only informs the reader, but also conditions the situations in which readers encounter blog content, moving between blogs in an open ended form of enquiry as they pursue an argument or line of reasoning.

As with the social networking site, therefore, a surface evaluation of individual blogs might encourage a negative view of something that produces banal, poor quality and sometimes unsavoury content. However, a closer look at the tool itself reveals something far more meaningful and intriguing. At the heart of the blog is a way of writing that is at once *authentic*, in the sense that it engages an audience; *extendable*, in the sense that it can be connected to other blogs and truly *sociable* in the sense that it can connect to a wide community of potential readers and collaborators.

In addition to this, the blog can also empower children in activities that require interaction, by removing physical, social or environmental inhibitors. Problems with mobility, motor control or visual impairment can often be addressed through the use of computer equipment. Issues or labels that constrain children in classroom situations – perceived views of them by peers, perhaps, or other factors effecting self-esteem – can be rendered less intrusive. Personality traits like shyness become less of an obstacle to participation when interaction is removed into the less competitive realm of asynchronous communication (Garner and Gillingham 1996).

Finally blogs are also highly adaptable. As we shall see in more detail later, bloggers can work together in all sorts of ways, contributing to a single blog or maintaining a blog of their own, for example (Richardson 2006: 20–6). The teacher can also adopt a number of different roles in relation to conduct on the blog moulding their little corner of the blogosphere to their very own specialised and – if necessary – private purposes. In fact given the simplicity of the fundamental technology that underpins the blog – the fact that material can be created in a content editor and then automatically converted into web content in a single simple process – the uses to which blogs can be put are numerous.

Wikis

This leads us to consider the wiki, for the same technological principle underpins this technology too. Put simply the wiki is a website that can be edited by any of its readers using a content editor similar to that employed by the blogger. However, the wiki moves us from the realm of simple participation to that of active collaboration. We have already come across one very famous example of a wiki in Wikipedia and this provides an excellent starting point for the present discussion. Wikipedia serves this purpose ideally because it exemplifies the character and purpose of the tool and inspires negative as well as positive connotations.

As a form of encyclopaedia, Wikipedia pages all conform to a standard template, incorporating images, text and hypertext. They also conform to a certain style in terms of presentation and language, although standards of execution do vary. As a wiki, Wikipedia is authored by the community of readers. New pages are being created all the time and all existing pages can be updated and extended. A number of organisations, many led by academic institutions, have grown up to oversee the creation and maintenance of certain pages or groups of pages and a classification system has been established in order to encourage certain standards in terms of citation, argumentation and presentation. Much of the content on Wikipedia is subject to scrutiny, therefore, but the fundamental principle of a resource that is authored and maintained by the community remains.

Despite its very significant achievement (at the last count there were nearly 3.5 million articles on the English Wikipedia site alone), Wikipedia is regularly vilified. Academics and publishers point to the essentially un-moderated character of Wikipedia and its limitations as a research tool. Many wiki pages are incomplete, in the sense that they only reflect one point of view or fail to tackle their subject in depth. Some pages are simply out of date or inaccurate and one occasionally encounters information, or mis-information, that has been introduced mischievously. As a rule of thumb one is probably wise to say that Wikipedia is a good place to start an enquiry, but a very bad place to conclude one, but this is not the place to explore this debate.

As with the blog, the fact that anyone can author or contribute to a wiki is both a weakness and a strength, but looking from the outside the weaknesses are more apparent (Stacy 2006: para. 25sqq; Rosenzweig 2006: 125–36). As critics are at pains to point out, an information environment that privileges the interested but poorly informed and relatively inarticulate amateur over the trained professional expert might seem more democratic, but is likely to lead to an aggregate impoverishment of knowledge and understanding. We might now be able to access more information more easily, but is the information we receive of a high quality and how is the uninformed person meant to distinguish the good from the bad? This is an important debate, but it is one that is focused on content and serves only to distract us from the tool.

At the heart of the wiki is the edit button, the tool that converts the webpage into a document and calls up the tool bars that allow us to edit it. This is how the web is converted from a read only to a read and write environment. However, there is much more to the wiki than this. Look closely at any Wikipedia page and you will see that you have access to other facilities, including a discussion board and a history tool. The discussion board allows people to share opinions or submit information about the page without actually editing it, while the history button allows readers to track back through all the different stages of its creation. This places the content itself in a discursive environment and renders all aspects of the wiki-page's construction and authorship transparent.

Leave aside the analysis of existing wiki content and look at the tools objectively, then, and you are left with an environment in which both teachers and children can create content on the web and use the internet to share that content widely (Richardson 2006: 66–7). Since wikis can contain the full range of multimedia resources they offer opportunities for presenting the fruits of many different activities, deriving from classroom based scenarios or from outside school. However, in addition to allowing children to share their work across the web, the wiki allows multiple authors to collaborate in the production of a page. One aspect of this collaboration that is often overlooked is the potential for cooperation between teacher and pupil, the fact that a wiki allows the teacher to create spaces on the web that are very precisely customised to a specific learning outcome. Some of our suggested activities build on this principle.

In addition to this, by virtue of the discussion board, the role and indeed the immediate presence of an audience enhances the wiki as a learning tool in similar ways to those described in relation to the blog. The fact that a wider community is able to comment, discuss and even add to and extend the resource has the potential to enhance the relevance of learning activities and the fact that this can happen over time helps establish learning in an environment that encourages reflection.

Podcasting and media sharing

All the tools discussed so far exploit the power of multimedia to create essentially new patterns of expression, encouraging children to develop forms of literacy in which sophisticated combinations of text, image audio and video can be used in order to convey meaning. However, it is a feature of all these tools that they take the website as their platform or template and share little with that other ubiquitous medium, television. Traditionally television or 'broadcasting' was the exclusive domain of specialist organisations that commanded very considerable financial clout and technical expertise. The problem was distribution, of course. Making a television programme was not technically difficult and in recent years domestic camcorders have become more affordable, easier to use and are technically more sophisticated. Actual broadcasting on the other hand depends upon expensive cable networks or Ultra High Frequency signals and the means of distribution is highly restricted. However, now – as in so many other realms – the internet offers an alternative method of distribution and in enters the podcast.

As with other Web 2.0 tools that have enabled wider access to traditionally closed forms of information and media production, the podcast is popularly associated with a process of 'dumbing-down'. The first podcasts tended to reside alongside more substantial media broadcasts and were condensed summaries of more substantial offerings. Subsequently the podcast was further diminished in the eyes of people involved in the media industry as freebies that would be offered to attract viewers to websites or to advertise other forms of media output. Seen as marketing tools or free offerings, podcasts have therefore suffered the perception that they are the inferior partner to broadcasts, based on qualitative comparisons to the more traditional forms of media production that they were intended to serve. Again content is allowed to define the tool in ways that make it look unsuitable for education.

In fact the term podcast is revealing since it refers only to the means by which the resource is distributed and says nothing about the content. In fact a podcast could consist of virtually anything that incorporates an audio or video recording. In practice we now encounter podcasts as substitutes for radio, television, audio guides, presentations, instruction manuals and more or less anything else that you could imagine somebody downloading from the internet in order to play back later for their information, edification or entertainment. Perhaps only one aspect of the podcast's rather unfortunate reputation is really justified and that is its cheapness. In the second section of this book we will look at a number of occasions when it might be useful to create a podcast and in all cases a powerful justification can be provided by setting the impact of the finished article against the very low levels of cost and effort involved in producing it. At the same time we shall see that the popularity and accessibility of media sharing platforms provide a powerful way for pupils to share their work with a wider audience to consume material from a wider learning community.

Web aggregators and social bookmarking

Other tools that require consideration at this stage are the social bookmarking and syndication tools, facilities like RSS and Delicious, which allow us to personalise and structure our interaction with the World Wide Web. As we shall see these tools have the potential to play a significant role in learning and it is not difficult to envisage a role for them in many of the classroom ideas or in relation to some of the case studies introduced in the next section. However, it would be wrong to imply that these tools have started to impact on primary teaching to the extent that the technologies examined above have done. Nevertheless it is important to consider them in the context of this book for two reasons. First they are likely to emerge as important tools in the near future, becoming a significant aid to the primary learner in their interaction with the web and, second, because they should be of immediate interest to the teacher who can use them to enhance professional practice.

RSS aggregators are simple tools, often embedded into standard web browsers, which allow us to subscribe to web content via 'feeds' so that new content from all over the web can be consolidated and made available at a single accessible location. Wherever you see the distinctive orange RSS symbol or encounter an invitation to take up a 'feed', you can quickly create a link to that site and have new content delivered to your aggregator automatically. This is most commonly available where information is updated regularly, sites containing blogs, for example, or those dealing with news or creative media.

Social bookmarking sites allow you to create annotated lists of favourites that can be accessed from any internet connection, not just one designated computer. Social bookmarks can be easily shared, therefore, and can be developed collaboratively. In addition to this it is possible to annotate your lists and to search other people's collections of favourites, providing a effective means of identifying useful content on the web. It is also worth noting at this stage that both RSS and social bookmarking provide teachers with a means of creating a filtered portal to the web.

A little earlier on we mentioned the issue of discriminating between good and bad content on the web. We asked, how newcomers to a field of knowledge, learners in other words, distinguished between good and bad information. The typical way of searching for web content is to use a search engine like AltaVista, Google or Yahoo. However, while search engines are getting more and more sophisticated and increasingly sensitive to individual preferences, the results they produce reflect the unstructured nature of the internet and their own commercial nature.

As commercial tools, search engines prioritise commercial sites and it can hardly escape the notice of any user that most of the results of a casual web-search lead to pages that are trying to sell something. This can introduce problems for schools as search engines can quickly expose users to inappropriate content, even if filters and age restricted settings are applied. Equally worrying, however, is this question of information quality, a situation that derives from the way the internet is structured, or not structured as is actually the case. Fundamental to the principle of the internet and enshrined in its architecture is the fact that the internet makes no judgement about the quality of information; it does not attempt to classify, but simply breaks large chunks of information up into manageable little parcels and sends them from one location to another. As a result, when a search engine pulls out information in response to a keyword search, none of the criteria it uses in prioritising results has much of a bearing on quality.

Most children learn strategies for identifying relevant content and schools teach children a number of tricks and strategies for locating and evaluating information, but few of these solutions even start to address the fundamental unstructured nature of the internet. This is where the aggregator and the social bookmarking site come in, for if the internet itself does not separate the wheat from the chaff then the individual user or the community of users will have to do so. The web aggregator allows the teacher to create a searchable database of web materials, while the social bookmarking site provides an environment in which children can be encouraged to evaluate websites according to a number of internal and external criteria. We shall develop these points, but it is worth noting that both of these processes are addressed in practical tasks below.

The main problem with the web aggregator is the terminology, which does little to demystify the underlying technology. Acronyms like RSS are hardly made less daunting when they are revealed, confusingly, to mean either really simple syndication or rich site summary. The term aggregator itself sounds like a specialist or technical term and, generally speaking, setting yourself up with your first feeds can feel like a daunting process. However, the aggregator allows the teachers and children to create a selective view of the internet without losing its essential dynamic quality. The users of a web aggregator continue to see new content and changes to their chosen pages as it appears or when they happen, but they are able to explore a carefully selected cross section of web content without being distracted by a morass of irrelevant or inappropriate material.

Similarly, social bookmarking can feel like a tremendous effort initially, but it requires only a small conceptual leap to translate these tools into an educational context. Creating bookmarks involves precisely the stages and skills that we require children to apply and develop as they interact with material on the web. They are required to classify the site according to its origin and purpose and make judgements about the quality of the content. Of course this latter part of the process is hard for the learner and requires children to compare sites, in order to identify the tell tale signs that mark out the good from the potentially misleading. Here the community dimension of the social bookmarking site can lend tangible assistance without compromising the learner's essential autonomy.

As with the discussion on social networking sites, the use of social bookmarking is yet to impact on teaching in the primary classroom. In reality very few pupils use these tools routinely. However, the potential for high quality learning particularly in the area of digital literacy should not be denied. Involving children in activities like classification and evaluation of information, whether it is from a hard copy text book or from online information, would be a desirable skill-set to be developed in pupils. Similarly the use of RSS and web aggregators in order to create selective views of web content are likely have a more prominent place in primary education as the knowledge and skills involved are commonplace. In the meantime it is imperative for teachers to develop their own skills and knowledge in this area in order to enhance their professional effectiveness in relation to online content.

Conclusion

In this chapter, then, we have applied the process of 're-thinking' that we introduced in the Introduction. We suggested that re-thinking involves separating our views of the tools themselves from the opinions we have developed from our encounters with the content they produce in recreational contexts. This is difficult because we rarely encounter these tools in any other context and we are, in any case, far more sensitive and alert to the content, or the 'message' – as McLuhan would have characterised it (McLuhan 1964) – than we are to the means by which it was produced. Part of the appeal of the internet is the ease with which we can access content without ever having to consider how it got there, after all. However, if we want to use these tools to our own advantage then we need to come to a much clearer view of their nature and their potential.

We have therefore defined some of the key tools in terms that make their application to learning comprehensible. We have presented social networking tools in a way that emphasises their potential for creating child centred and highly personalised learning environments. Blogs have been described in terms that highlight their potential to draw out children's creative potential, while wikis are introduced as a medium in which children can collaborate and be introduced to new roles, as producers and publishers of knowledge. We have encouraged the reader to think about podcasts as something that children could create and share, rather than simply consume and have discussed the ways in which RSS and social bookmarking might help to support enquiry and exploration on the web. We probably have some way to go before we can say that we have proved our case, but this process is an essential first step towards that goal.

Practical tasks

In order to use these tools it is important to understand them and this involves exploring them on an operational as well as a conceptual level. The best way to achieve this is to get stuck in and 'have a go'.

1   Use a search engine to identify sites that allow you to create a blog and a wiki. Sites that the authors of this book have used include Wordpress.com and Blogger.com for blogs and wikispaces.com or pbworks.com for wikis. Create one of each type of site using the support provided by the sites themselves. Experiment with adding some content to the site and remember to make a note of your login details as it will be useful to be able to return to these tools later in the book.
2   If you have not done so already create an account on any of the popular social networking sites. You do not have to disclose anything about yourself or invite anyone to join your network, but it is useful to get a feel of the environment and its potential.
3   Join YouTube and note how easy it is to upload video. If you have access to a flip camera or have a mobile phone or media device that produces video in Mp4 format you will find that you can upload these files directly to the site.
4   Go to Google and click on the blue link at the top of the page that reads 'More'. Scan down the list that appears and click 'Reader'. Read the blurb on that page and click the link that reads 'take the tour' in order to find out more about how RSS and aggregators work. A good starting point is to search the web for news sites that are appropriate for children. Go to the BBC 'News-round' site, weekly reader.com and Sciencenewsforkids. org. In each case find the RSS feed and paste the link for that page into your reader. Then use the tools on your Google reader page to search and explore the content you have subscribed to.
5   Sign up with delicious.com and if you have access to a computer of your own install the 'Delicious toolbar'. You are now ready to start bookmarking the web socially. A good place to start is with your own list of 'favourites' or 'bookmarks'. Access each in turn from your browser and use the delicious toolbar to add them to your social bookmarks. Finally return to Delicious and look at how your list looks there. Note how many other people have chosen to include the same sites as you in their list.

Chapter 2

Web 2.0 and barriers in the primary classroom

This chapter addresses the following themes:

- problems associated with the teaching of ICT;
- problems linked to using Web 2.0 in the classroom;
- topical discussions on the advantages and disadvantages of using the internet in the classroom;
- internet safety;
- a strategy for developing responsible users of new technology.

There have been numerous cumulative changes to the curriculum over the last decade and the resulting system of education makes many demands on teachers who report difficulties in delivering the required skills and content. Over the same period we have witnessed rapid advances in web technologies and teachers have been expected to reflect this in their practice as well. In particular, these developments have added new impetus to ideas about the place of ICT as a curriculum subject, culminating in the recommendations made by both Rose (2009) and Alexander (Alexander and Flutter 2009).

Technological innovation has resulted in new opportunities and has offered approaches to learning that can be considered both creative and motivating in their curriculum application. Unfortunately, ICT in schools has traditionally been seen not so much as an opportunity for creativity, but as a problematic and somewhat burdensome curriculum subject. Although the main aim of this text is to explore some of the exciting new ways in which technology can be harnessed, time needs to be spent examining some of the issues that complicate the teaching of ICT.

Poor teacher confidence has long been associated with the delivery of the ICT curriculum. BECTA (2004) has explored this issue and concludes that several distinct elements combine and accumulate to make this subject particularly difficult for teachers. Some of the problems typically expressed by practitioners that cause poor confidence include a lack of access to technology, both at home and in the professional arena, and a lack of technical support.

Much has been implemented in the last decade to rectify the problem of access for both pupils and teachers, with government initiatives allocating monies purely for the purpose of upgrading hardware and providing fast broadband connections. However, the issue of resourcing would appear to be an ongoing problem that has not been satisfactory resolved. A recent survey carried out by BESA (British Educational Suppliers Association) in 2009, involving 770 primary schools and 572 secondary schools, revealed some worrying trends. Not least of all, more than 80 per cent of teachers claimed that limited access to ICT affected their use of it in the classroom. Worse, when considering the development of Web 2.0 applications, the survey revealed that primary pupil access to the internet, which stood at 73 per cent in 2006, had declined to 58 per cent in 2009.

Understanding and delivering effective ICT lessons also requires that a certain amount of time be dedicated to the preparation and planning of activities and teachers need to ensure that they are confident in their use of the technologies that they intend to use. This time is often difficult to come by when added to all the other curriculum pressures faced by a teacher and the problem is compounded by the need to set time aside within lessons involving technology in order to set up equipment and to ensure that it is working.

What is more, questions about reliability frequently make teachers feel uneasy and fear that the technology will let them down or even not work at all. Ultimately, BECTA (2004) suggest that the investment of required time when planning for ICT can appear too onerous in relation to the perceived benefits to the learning experience of the children. The same publication suggests that the problems of time and resources listed above only address some of the surface issues associated with the dilemmas that ICT can present. A more deep seated factor responsible for scepticism towards ICT appears to be due to the inherently slow nature of educational change. Educationalists were found to be generally 'resistant' to change and particularly so in the case of ICT use (BECTA 2004). This is, perhaps, understandable, given the pressures that teachers face in delivering a packed and expanding curriculum and given the risk-averse culture imposed by league tables. Nevertheless, the suspicion remains that barriers like those already mentioned are compounded and reinforced by an institutionalised resistance to new strategies and new methods of delivering the curriculum using ICT.

Using technology can require teachers to move from their preferred styles of delivery and relinquish tried and tested strategies that they feel confident with. Incorporating new techniques involves a certain amount of risk taking and this can sit uncomfortably with practitioners when it is children's learning that appears to be at stake. Adopting new styles of teaching is a slow process and Kennewell (2006) sympathises with this problem when discussing the new opportunities offered by interactive whiteboards. He points out that interactive whiteboards have been a characteristic feature of most primary classrooms for several years now, but that the potential of the boards for improving delivery via interactive and dialogic approaches has 'stalled' at the stage of 'surface interactivity' (Kennewell 2006).

While the best practitioners are described as achieving rich learning experiences, many use the same technologies in a limited, didactic fashion. The limited nature of pedagogical change is a concern of Kennewell's (2006) paper and exemplifies the problems associated with transforming teaching practices via the use of technology. In a similar vein, Cox *et al.* (2000) found that there has been a longstanding problem with the ICT training given to teachers in the UK. They found that it has mostly concentrated on the technical skills associated with running software and using hardware and failed to develop the same level of understanding about the creative teaching and learning opportunities afforded by technology.

BECTA (2004) agree with this, stating that despite an enormous effort to improve teacher competence in the UK, including national training programmes, the outcomes have been varied. For instance, the 1998 DfES initiated National Grid for Learning Strategy established the New Opportunities Fund programme which sought to improve the delivery of ICT. The resulting learning package was comprehensive, but focused on the acquisition of competences that were arguably of limited use and somewhat over-whelming in their presentation. The density of learning tasks to be tackled and conquered diverted attention away from the creative potential of ICT.

It could be said that teachers will only change their ICT practice if they believe in the benefits it gives to children and that this depends on a good pedagogical under-standing as well as skills development. Before using technology, practitioners need to examine 'why' they are doing so, otherwise the use of ICT can result in the blind application of software to meet a need that has been prescribed by a higher authority or curriculum document (Wild 1996). Initial teacher training tutors should also focus on pedagogical understanding, particularly in relation to Web 2.0 activities, as well as the application of skills in order for good practice to be embedded across the profession. The theme of pedagogical application will be the mainstay of the next chapter of this book.

For many teachers, the problems of ICT teaching can be exacerbated by the knowl-edge that the children they teach may know more than they do. The teacher can fear the potential for humiliation when using new technologies in front of the class and may be concerned about retaining control in an environment that the children find more congenial than the teacher. This sense is frequently unfounded or at least exaggerated in the mind of the teacher, but a recent review of child safety on the internet provides an interesting perspective on this issue.

Byron (2008) discusses a relevant aspect of the digital divide, suggesting that one of the reasons for parents being concerned about children using Web 2.0 resources is due to the fact that they are largely ignorant of what their children are experiencing and so cannot use their own personal narrative and understanding to guide their children correctly. This concept can be equally applied to the educational establishment. Teachers are traditionally used to being the person who 'knows' the answers, or if they do not know the answers they are better equipped than their pupils to find them out. When discussing technology, this comfortable situation does not necessarily apply.

It is quite likely that at least some children in a class will be quite sophisticated users of technology and, even if they are not more competent in their use of it than the tea-cher, they are likely to be more inclined to adopt a playful approach to using equip-ment. However, although the concerns associated with this must be acknowledged, there are significant opportunities here as well.

Lord Puttnam (2008), chair of Futurelab (an organisation dedicated to transforming teaching and learning through the innovative use of new technologies) articulates this conundrum well. He asserts that children of the digital age can frequently demonstrate the effective use of technology, not only to their peers but also to their teachers. He acknowledges that this shift in practice is entirely 'counter-cultural' to more traditional notions of what a teacher should be and how they might normally dominate the learning in a classroom. Only the most confident primary school teachers are able to use the potential of pupils in this way without being worried about loss of status. However, he observes that this can provide a very powerful learning medium that should be taken advantage of.

While the above paragraphs have discussed barriers towards the uptake of ICT in general, there are concerns about this particular learning environment provided by the

World Wide Web that need to be examined further. While many web-based activities are potentially exciting, it cannot be denied that recognition of the opportunities for learning has to be balanced with an awareness of some of the associated dangers of participation in online activities.

Byron (2008) suggests that there are several characteristics peculiar to the web that might be seen as having the potential for harm. There is little doubt that it can increase a child's likelihood of encountering inappropriate language or content of a sexual or violent nature. She examines the potential for harm to children from exposure to inappropriate materials and concludes that there is a small but accumulating body of evidence suggesting a link between exposure to sexually explicit materials and negative beliefs and attitudes. Although schools now utilise filtering software in order to protect children from obscene and abusive content, the issue of complete protection presents an ongoing problem, particularly when we consider that children are using the web at home as well.

Another risk, but one that receives less attention than that presented by sexual and violent material, is that of inappropriate commercial content, for the web is cluttered with a diverse array of unmonitored advertising. Byron (2008) examines the ability of children to filter and discern the difference between genuine web content and materials that are commercial in nature. She fears that children are not developmentally mature enough to notice diverse material types and are therefore unable to decipher different types of messages. She reasons that it is only when children reach early adulthood that the brain becomes sophisticated enough to determine the many purposes of web content. Some websites could also be accused of reinforcing stereotypical images to impressionable young children and do not offer enough diversity.

One of the biggest 'dangers' of the internet has to be the potential for children to meet others and the opportunity for strangers to falsify their identity. Children need to be aware of the risks they face if they give out personal information on the web and the potential for information they disclose online to fall into the wrong hands. Clearly, the web has provided a new avenue for paedophiles to make contact with and groom potential victims. There are instances that have been well documented by the media involving children and teenagers who have become victims of abuse where initial contact was made via a social networking site; the aggressor usually having lied about their circumstances and their reasons for making that initial contact.

Byron (2008) also suggests that another type of contact risk associated with social networking sites centres on the way that children are grouped without consideration for age. This 'vertical age-grouping' could provide new potential for inappropriate contact and potential avenues for cyber bullying (Byron 2008: 53). While the advent of cyber bullying is still less prevalent than more traditional forms of bullying, it can present a more insidious and persistent threat to the victim as it has the potential to pervade every area of a child's life. If a child was being bullied at school, the victim could traditionally find short-lived relief from the situation within the sanctuary of the home. With cyber bullying the perpetrator has the opportunity to infiltrate both home and school life via the use of technology and distribute malicious material about their victim to a much wider audience. While verbal bullying is extremely unpleasant for the victim, the spoken word can be more quickly forgotten than material that lingers on the web forum on which it was presented.

Another widely voiced concern of parents is the amount of time young users spend playing games and the implications of screen time for the health and well being of a child. Prensky (2003) details some interesting data on the activities of children and states that by the time they reach the age of 21, the average student will have spent 10,000 hours playing computer games and over 10,000 hours talking on digital cell phones. Seib (2010) discusses the emergence of a new type of 'screen' addiction in children and examples of excessive game playing are likened to obsessive behaviours. She states that such games are particularly addictive to young men who struggle to fit in with social norms and find access to status and a form of popularity online that is denied them in the embodied world. In this situation game playing becomes intrinsically rewarding and Seib points to research that suggests that some children and young adults are recorded as spending up to 17 hours a day playing online games like World of Warcraft and EverQuest. During this time players are likely to exhibit addictive behaviours like not observing mealtimes or skipping homework. She also points to extreme cases of young men dying in internet cafés in Asia after gaming sessions that lasted up to 86 hours.

Byron (2008) discusses screen addiction and video game playing in some detail. She concludes that actually very few children fit the criteria for true addiction, but the excessive time children spend playing could be seen as a cause for concern. She also discusses the possibility of violent game playing leading to more aggressive behaviours in children, although the lack of longitudinal studies into the impact of video gaming on child development is acknowledged. Nevertheless, on this point the report concludes that most researchers consulted during the study believed that there is some kind of effect of inappropriate content on some children in some contexts and circumstances.

O'Brien (2008) also discusses the issue of prolonged use of technology in relation to gaming and general online activity, but extends discussion to include concerns about how technology might be changing the way we think and learn. She reviews the way the younger 'Google generation' learn by collating information from multiple sources and concludes that, while children and young adults might be able to absorb information quickly, they lack reflective and critical awareness. She likens this to 'bouncing' or 'flicking' behaviour which results in learners using electronic information sources in a 'horizontal' form rather than in a deeper, 'vertical', manner. Users tend to use websites, she concludes, in superficial ways rather than for sustained thinking.

Ziegler (2007) examines the cumulative effects of many forms of media, particularly their impact on the development of children and young adults. The same author acknowledges the potential of tools like Facebook to 'better motivate students as engaged learners rather than learners who are primarily passive observers of the educational process' (ibid.: 69), but argues that the potentially harmful effect of technology is realised when 'heavy' media users adopt the social realities portrayed by it. The world of young adults today is not only defined by the voices of parents, peers and the world of school, but also by faceless people in the world of cyberspace who may present or verify information in an undesirable fashion. In the past, it was argued, the 'Pied Pipers' influencing children could be easily identified, something that is no longer possible to the same degree.

In fact a number of educationalists have voiced general concerns about the state of childhood today and the role that media and ICT have played in this. Influential among these voices is that of Palmer, who cites electronic media as one of the elements responsible for creating a 'toxic childhood' (Palmer 2006). Although she acknowledges that technology can be a vibrant resource for children, Palmer also points out some of the pitfalls, suggesting that the use of technology can cause children to retreat into their own solitary virtual world, thereby losing opportunities for 'real' play. At the same time a reliance on media led activities is associated with an increase in bad eating habits (solitary snacking) and a lack of sleep caused by the distractions presented by electronic equipment in a child's room (ibid.).

In a later book Palmer extends her argument to cover the impact of technology on young children and their capacity to learn. She suggests that learning to read involves a slowing down of the mind in order to process sounds into words, which can be contrasted to the use of technology which may speed up the mind and can be associated with 'quick fix' types of learning (Palmer 2008). Of course Palmer's views, along with those found in much of the literature cited so far, may be seen to be directed at inappropriate uses of ICT and the web, rather than at the essential character or potential of the tools themselves. However, she has constructed powerful arguments around the ways in which technology can become a default activity and how it can fill space at the expense of family life. Acts like checking emails and other forms of electronic correspondence are presented as activities that exhibit elements of compulsive behaviour. When a user logs on to a computer or checks their mobile phone they cannot know whether an email or a text message is waiting for them and are therefore likely to see one as a form of reward or affirmation. She notes how intermittent rewards like those offered by electronic tools can make for compulsive usage and can therefore hold greater short-term appeal than interaction with more stable and routine relations such as those encountered within the family, which can therefore be taken for granted.

Similar views are also found in both academic and popular literature from fields other than education. For example, Professor Greenfield has recently written of her fears for children learning through a screen based environment: in a book (Greenfield 2008) and several newspaper articles released at around the same time (e.g. Greenfield 2009). In these contexts she argues that the use of electronic media for children distorts their perceptions of reality and diminishes their capacity for empathy. On one level Greenfield's arguments are scientific and grounded in neuroscience. She postulates that excessive dopamine production, stimulated by addictive game playing causes dysfunctional behaviour in the frontal cortex resulting in a loss of attention span and other sorts of behaviours that compromise learning. Her principal conclusion is delivered in the form of a call for further research into the effect of computing on the brain. However, her argument is also eminently well suited to less specialised forums as well. Not only has Greenfield found a ready audience in the popular press, but her work has stimulated a considerable volume of journalism as well (Cornwall 2008; Craig 2009).

To a certain extent this is a direct result of Greenfield's own emphatic and colourful style, which is frequently uncompromising and uses memorable expressions, such as her allusions to 'the yuk and wow generation' (Greenfield 2009b). Her work reads easily within a popular context and has wide appeal. However, Greenfield is not the only scientist working in this area whose work has stimulated wider interest in the negative impacts of technology on children. For example, a letter printed in the *The Daily Telegraph* in 2006, entitled 'Modern life leads to more depression among children' (Abs *et al.* 2006) voiced the concern of a number of academics, and professionals about the relationship between aspects of modern life, new media among them, and increasing levels of drug dependence and depression in young people.

This letter pointed to several factors that could be responsible for this, including an overly academic, test driven curriculum, a competitive culture and the increasing prominence of the media and the internet in children's lives. Like Greenfield they conclude with a call for a public debate on the matter and the popular press can be seen to have responded, driven in large part by a UNICEF report of 2007, which placed Britain at the bottom of a table of 21 developed countries for child welfare. This was judged according to a number of measures including education, health and family relationships and, despite government claims that the information was out of date, its dramatic conclusions are impossible to ignore.

However, despite the wide ranging and very serious implications of the UNICEF report for our understanding of the problems facing many children in areas such as their family life and access to basic public services, the popular media's interest in child welfare has tended to focus on the less well defined and more general arena of 'modern life', whether this is explored in the form of the impact of media on self-image and the premature sexualisation of children or the impact of computer games and social networking on more traditional forms of play. In this respect therefore, it can be seen to be preoccupied with a much more generalised question of what 'childhood' should be, a recurring issue that causes anxiety in every generation.

Recent examples of reporting in this vein include broadcasts such as ITV1's three part series 'Tonight' (2011) reported in the *Daily Telegraph* on 02 January 2011 (Etchingham 2011). This series travelled the country examining negative experiences of childhood and targeted issues from the impact of media on body image and sedentary lifestyles and the role of the curriculum and testing on mental health. Prominent in the reporting of this programme and highlighted in the broadcast itself was a survey of parents which identified strong feelings that children did not play outside for long enough, that work precluded sufficient 'family time', that television promoted poor self-esteem through the depiction of unattainable models of physical attractiveness. It was also concluded that the internet exacerbated children's problems in a generalised sense.

Ultimately, while there are clearly considerable social problems facing children today and although many appear to be being failed by institutions such as schools, the themes that appear to resonate most with journalists and the wider audience centre around a far less well defined discomfort with the lifestyles of children, which are – to no small extent due to the role of media and the internet in their lives – very different from the experience of their parents. Certainly the kind of 'public' debate called for by Greenfield and the letter writers cited above – a serious exploration of the impact of modern life on children and its relationship to the kinds of trends identified in the UNESCO report – has not taken place.

That is not to say that there is no debate and there are voices that seek to present a balancing point of view, such as Alexander (2008), who calls for a re-examination of the nature of childhood in the twenty-first century. Although reporting the problems of curriculum overload and pressures on children, he does present a more buoyant view of a child's life in the UK. He reports that many children were noticeably positive about their lives when questioned directly and that the most strongly stated concerns were expressed by adults on their children's behalf. He argues for a move away from alarmist views by stating that the cultural construct of childhood should shift from that of seeing children as helpless victims to one where children are 'empowered' and which builds on what children can do as learners and social beings.

Byron (2008) looks more specifically at how to prepare children to use electronic media in a safe manner, but adopts the same tone as Alexander, by encouraging an objective view of the subject matter. She discusses how the 'focus' on some of the most undesirable aspects of the web has 'skewed' the debate on using this kind of technology and that negative views have been over-emphasised. In doing so she uses the same language of 'empowerment' when using the web in relation to children, and comes to a similar conclusion to that of Alexander (2008). In each case these authors can be seen to present children as agents in the solution to the challenges they encounter in modern life, emphasising the need to provide them with the skills and the personal resources to operate safely and constructively within their real world and virtual environments.

Web safety: recommendations for children and young people – what practitioners need to know

Byron (2010: 11) discusses several ways that children can become aware of the risks when using Web 2.0 products, but, ultimately, she advocates supporting children to become 'savvy internet users'. A summary of some of her recommendations will be presented below alongside some practical tasks to carry out. It is worth focusing on her conclusions for a moment, which are presented concisely in the executive summary. Byron observes that the potential of the internet, to empower children and to promote personal development and learning is grounded in the same fundamental attributes of the network that create the dangers outlined above. One cannot, to state the problem clearly, obviate the dangers of the web without diminishing its positive potential as well. In this sense then she likens learning to use the internet to other activities, like crossing the road, which present serious hazards, but are instrumental in widening the child's personal horizons.

Within this same discussion of internet safety, Byron (2008) states that there needs to be a shift in people's understanding of their role in keeping children safe online. All adults involved in the care and education of children must be proactive about safety and not simply reactive to an incident after it has taken place. She calls this moving the mindset from a state of pre-contemplation (not engaging or thinking about the issue) to a state of contemplation (deciding to engage with the issue at hand). Following her final report, the New Labour government of the time agreed to implement her recommendations and a multi-stakeholder UK Council for Child Internet Safety (UKCCIS) was established. One of its prime tasks was to raise awareness of internet safety so that there was a quick change in perceptions of how to tackle the problems presented by this new technology.

Online features that raise awareness of risk

Most educational establishments will be employing some sort of filtering mechanism that blocks unsuitable content for children; this is usually provided by the local authority. From experience it can be stated that filtering systems can be unwieldy to use with time having to be spent waiting for the local authority or an Internet Service Provider to give access to a site so that it can be used. This can be frustrating for both teacher and pupils. Using filtering systems can also restrict the opportunity for enquiry and collaboration, the very heart of Web 2.0 potential. Filtering systems, therefore, do offer much protection from harm but they do not represent an all encompassing solution to e-safety and they do have some problems associated with their use.

OFSTED (2010) found that the schools that were best at providing e-safety training were not those which used systems that were totally 'locked down' but instead used 'managed systems', which have fewer inaccessible sites and less filtering imposed on them. Children using 'locked down' systems were ultimately more vulnerable as they had less knowledge of how to protect themselves from risk (OFSTED 2010). Children do not only use the internet in school but also use it in a variety of other locations as well, where much more liberal filtering may be applied. It is worth considering other approaches and possible solutions to promote e-safety.

Practical task 1

In the educational establishment where you are employed or conducting work experience, find out what sort of filtering mechanism is used. Try accessing some Web 2.0 tools like Flickr or YouTube. Were you given access to these sites or was it restricted?

In your educational establishment find and the read the policy that discusses web access for children. Consider:

- when the policy was formulated or last reviewed;
- if the policy reflects the changing nature of the web and if it assesses the new potential risks presented by Web 2.0 tools;
- whether the policy is adequate or if more changes are required.

Internet search engines are one of the most commonly used tools on the web. Byron (2008) points out that most search engines actually include a 'safe search option', which can act as a filtering system. However, this facility usually has to be activated by a user as most search engines have their safety tools set at a 'moderate' and therefore relatively permissive level. Byron (2008) recommends that public awareness of this option should be raised and that it should be made more obvious how to use this facility. Practitioners certainly need to be aware of tools like this when considering e-safety.

Practical task 2

Look at some different search engines and consider the following:

- how do you activate the 'safe search option'?
- how easy is it to access?
- how many clicks away from the first page do you have to make before this feature is located?
- are the safety options well signposted from the initial page?

Byron (2008) does not advocate that search engines should automatically have their safety settings set at the highest level and argues that the emphasis should be on users changing the setting themselves. Why do you think she has decided this? Do you agree with this particular line of thought?

Many websites are now issuing an age-verification requirement before giving access to their content. This kind of facility provides another preventative layer for children and adults warning them that they might encounter unsuitable content. The actual purpose and value given to these types of features is debatable. After all, it is very easy for children and adults to lie about their age when registering and usually access is given to a site after the mere ticking of a box. Byron (2008) examines this issue and discusses the problems associated with age-verification. She calls for the methods employed for age verification to be improved and to be continuously reviewed.

Practical task 3

Discuss the point of having age-verification requirements on websites. Do they have any purpose? How successful do you think they are in restricting access to content? What is the philosophy behind warning notices like these?

Raising awareness in children

Byron (2010: 11) seeks to identify clear digital safety information for children. She uses the term 'resilience' in her language here, a term which is a very worthwhile one. The word 'resilience' is widely used and recognised by practitioners when considering the social and emotional development of very young learners. The *Practice Guidance for the Early Years Foundation Stage* (DCSF 2008) finds that those children who are secure in their emotional responses and in their social relationships with both their peers and with adults exhibit good 'resilience'. Children who have a resilient personality usually adapt better to change and new situations; they may be able to focus with more perseverance on their learning than children who are less stable. The term resilience is a good one to use in regard to e-safety and indeed 'digital resilience' is considered by Byron.

Byron (2010) has established a digital code and a set of behaviours called 'Zip It, Block It, Flag It' – this code needs to be used by practitioners with children.

- 'Zip It' relates to the idea – 'Keep your personal stuff private and think about what you say and do online'.
- 'Block It' relates to the idea – 'Block people who send nasty messages and don't open unknown links and attachments'.
- 'Flag It' relates to the idea – 'Flag up with someone you trust if anything upsets you or if someone asks to meet you offline'.

Practical task 4

As well as a digital code there is now an online resource that children can access in order to learn about digital safety. The resource, set up as the result of a collaboration between UKCCIS, the Teaching Development Agency, BECTA and the DCSF, is called Know it all and takes the form of an adventure game (SMART Adventure) through which children travel, learning about internet safety on the way.

Go to the Know it all website (<http://www.childnet-int.org/kia/primary/>) and look at the SMART adventure for primary school children. Consider the following:

- from which age group could this adventure be used?
- what type of follow up activities would you employ with the children?
- what key vocabulary would you want the children to learn as a result of watching this animation?
- what key questions might you ask the children?
- what prerequisite literacy skills do you think the children need in order to be able to access and understand the adventure?
- do you think the adventure would appeal to primary age children that may already be sophisticated media users and if so why is this?

Go to the QTS standards for trainee teachers at:
<http://www.tda.gov.uk/partners/ittstandards/guidance_08/qts.aspx>
Look at the standards and assess which one/s can be specifically linked to e-safety.

The Child Exploitation and Online Protection Centre (CEOP) is another online service that provides resources that educate children about the potential threats to be found on the internet. In particular, there is an area on the site dedicated especially to teacher development called 'Think U Know'. Of note is another online adventure game that is aimed at younger children in Key Stage 1.

Practical task 5

Go to the CEOP website and view the adventure animation aimed at Key Stage 1. http://www.thinkuknow.co.uk/. Consider the following:

- at what age do you think it suitable to start teaching children about e-safety?
- at what age do you think children should be able to use the internet without adult support?

The message that schools have a responsibility to teach e-safety awareness to children has quickly spread across educational communities. As explored above there are a number of online resources available that start to tackle the issue, but it is interesting to consider the different ways e-safety can be taught in school. The Byron Report (2008) emphasises that the potential benefits and risks on the internet are so closely entwined that one cannot obviate one without compromising the other. In this situation, as the report itself concludes, schools have an obligation to tackle the issue of e-safety *online,* conveying to children rules and strategies for behaving responsibly. Teaching e-safety without using the tools that children and young adults use for online activity could be construed as erroneous.

Practical task 6

As the messages concerning e-safety gain momentum, a common approach is to engage children in making posters and displays showing their knowledge of this issue. These activities are valuable and effective and should not be criticised. However, it is worthwhile to spend a little time thinking of more cross-curricular activities that could be used to promote children's understanding and awareness and the opportunities that using Web 2.0 tools might present. Remember Byron's analogy of crossing the road. It attempts to convey the principle that controlled exposure to risks presents the best way of mitigating them in the longer term. If we were to apply this same principle to e-safety we would need to think of ways of using Web 2.0 tools that promoted awareness of the risks inherent in their misuse and understanding of responsible behaviours.

Web 2.0 and professional identity: digital footprints

As well as educating children about the internet, all staff who work with children need to be up-to-date with e-safety issues. This does not just mean teachers themselves, but also teaching assistants and parental volunteers – people who frequently work with small groups of pupils. OFSTED (2010) found that support staff received little or no training on e-safety and when training did occur it focused on the task of relaying information about compliance with e-safety procedures rather than on how to teach pupils to adopt safe and responsible practices when using new technologies.

Reflection 1

Who should be responsible for e-safety training in a school?

All staff, not just teachers, need to be aware of the potential misuse of web tools. Moreover, teachers and helpers need to be aware of their own digital footprints and how these can be misused and abused to the detriment of their own professional standing. Staff need to be conscious that the content they upload to their social networking sites could portray them in an unprofessional light. They also need to understand how personal and professional boundaries can be breached, not only in their physical environment but also in their virtual world as well. Social networking provides a new way to keep in touch with friends and family and also opens up new avenues to meet new people. However, all staff that work with children need to ensure that their profiles on social networking sites have been established securely so that the information on them remains private. They need to ensure that they read privacy settings on the networks that are used and settings are changed to ensure photographs and text remain in the hands of only the people they have granted access to.

Reflection 2

Think about the social networking sites you use.

- as a teacher or a student teacher do you think it is acceptable to have parents of the children you teach as 'friends'?
- think about your own digital footprint – are you sure the content that represents you is secure?
- have you set up 'strong passwords' (for instance, a password that is a combination of letters, symbols and numbers) on your social networking sites?

- do you know if your profile is set to 'public' or 'private' on your social networking sites?
- is there content on your social networking sites that potentially could present you in an unfortunate light?
- do you think carefully before posting content on a social networking site?
- do you know how to report any concerns you have about misuse of content on your social networking sites?

Due to the nature of teaching, time spent talking to colleagues is often precious and at a premium. Frequently, time runs out and conversations are left unfinished as the need to get back to the classroom becomes overwhelming. It may be tempting to carry on those conversations virtually and it could be suggested that practitioners have to be very wary of letting dialogue of a professional nature overflow on to social networking sites no matter how secure they are thought to be.

Conclusion

This chapter has reviewed some of the barriers to learning with ICT. Technology and the use of it is an exciting way to learn although it does have some problems associated with it. Some of these difficulties have to be acknowledged and understood and we have seen authors like Palmer (2008) and Ziegler (2007) construct powerful arguments around the potential dangers that can follow from addictive uses of media technology and from careless use of the internet.

However, most of the authors cited above fall short of recommending that new media and internet technologies be banned from schools or from the curriculum. In fact Ziegler (2007) recommends that young learners should be educated in how to navigate through information and envisages an important role for schools in teaching responsible and constructive uses of web technology. Looking at the question of child safety and the ways in which this can be compromised by the internet, the thrust of the Byron Report (2008) is that the solution lies in education, not in excluding such technologies from education.

Web 2.0 offers potentially innovative learning opportunities, many of which will be explored in the following chapter. Alongside these new learning situations, new potential risks arise from inappropriate uses of technology. Game playing on computers is not inherently bad, but addictive game playing or playing games that bring children into contact with inappropriate material and situations is. In this context a discussion that does not simply explore how risks should be managed, but also examines how web tools can empower children as learners and supports their development as resilient and knowledgeable internet users is important. This is the subject of the next chapter.

Chapter 3

The role of social software in the classroom

This chapter attempts to establish a positive case for the use of social software.
The following topics are covered:

- the experiences and expectations of the child;
- the needs of modern day learners and the adults of tomorrow;
- the pedagogy of the social web.

Experiences and expectations

It is important to acknowledge that children do not come to school with a single set of experiences. Differences in social and cultural background influence the amount of exposure a child is likely to have had to computers and to the internet. Parental attitudes, which are also very varied, have a tremendous impact on the child's own views. Nevertheless, it is fair to say that many children are exposed to computers and the internet at a very early age and that experience provides them with certain expectations about the technologies that they encounter in school.

As children develop during their primary school years it is likely that they will acquire a range of skills in using computer technologies and the internet through a variety of recreational and social activities. Again, their precise experience will depend on a number of factors, but in many cases the internet plays a growing role as a medium through which children discover and come to know the world around them. For example, the internet overlaps with many of the recreational and cultural spheres in which children operate. It is a means of communication with relatives and friends, a place to play games and a means to find information about hobbies or interests. In fact, the distinction between the virtual and the 'real' is becoming blurred, as television programmes and many of the activities and products that children encounter in the embodied world create extensions in cyberspace, in the form of websites.

The fact that children acquire so much of their understanding of internet and computer technologies outside school can render the use of ICT in the classroom problematic. The child may associate the computer or the internet with recreational or sociable activities and therefore behave in ways that disrupt group work and undermine the more structured approach to learning and teaching encountered in school. They may even associate it with approaches to learning that undermine the kinds of activities undertaken in formal learning situations.

For example, we have already seen viewpoints that cast the role of ICT in children's lives as an essentially destructive influence, one that compromises the child's ability to succeed in formal learning situations. Proponents of this view equate overuse of the internet and excessive exposure to television with a reliance on surface learning and a lack of critical or reflective faculties. From their perspective, school acquires a role in countering the effects of a broad social malaise that affects development and manifests itself in children's approaches to the learning process (Palmer 2006; Greenfield 2008). We have already suggested that these arguments are misplaced, in that they define the technologies according to a narrow range of (mis)uses. Nevertheless, we have also acknowledged that these misuses are commonplace and do have significant consequences.

Seen in this way the obligation on schools is inverted, requiring them to engage with the tension between the electronic environment and the values of traditional education in order to create new opportunities for learning by engaging children in rigorous and critical uses of new media and the internet. This approach assumes that the internet and related communication technologies have the potential to enhance education, but acknowledges that there is a need to look critically at the gulf that exists between the uses of ICT that children encounter inside and outside school. There is clearly a need to address many of the practices and conventions associated with recreational uses of the web and the casual approaches to information and learning that have grown up around them. However, there may be areas in which we have to look carefully at some of the values that inform education with a view to testing their continued relevance. Perhaps we ought to look with dismay, rather than satisfaction, at the fact that ICT has impacted on learning much less markedly than on spheres of social, cultural and recreational activity (Torgerson and Zhu 2004).

As a number of commentators have been at pains to point out in recent years (Frechette 2002; Buckingham 2007), the reason for this discrepancy is as much to do with the structures and processes encountered in schools as it is with the technology itself. Children encounter technology as a 'cultural form' (Buckingham 2007), a medium that plays an integral part in the activities it supports and interacts with the information it conveys. It has directly contributed to the creation of new codes and language forms, for example, impacting on patterns of speech as well as written communication. Schools, on the other hand, define learning and teaching according to an essentially conservative and well established set of values and seek to use technology in the quest for traditionally defined goals. To continue our example, the patterns of speech that social and recreational uses of technology have fostered are generally prohibited and so by this and other means the computer and the internet are stripped of 'cultural meaning' in order to render them as 'neutral tools'.

On one level this is understandable. The fact that a tool is capable of doing something or that it is associated with certain practices in other contexts does not necessarily mean that one has to import those uses or practices into the classroom in order to justify its use. The fact that children are used to using abbreviations in electronic communication, for example, does not mean that normal conventions of writing need to be abandoned or that web-technologies cannot play an important role in teaching those conventions. Just as we have sought to redefine Web 2.0 tools in the first chapter, it is appropriate to rethink ways in which computers can be used and to set new standards for use in formal learning situations.

Nevertheless, it is important for schools to use technologies in ways that reflect their influence on a world that is increasingly shaped by electronic media and the internet. Children need to be able to engage with learning technologies as things that are relevant to them and have relevance outside the classroom environment. To this extent, at least, it is important to engage with the notion that computer and internet technologies are part of a broader cultural milieu in which children participate outside school and which is relevant to their learning in a number of different contexts. To continue our example about language, while we would be justified in banning many common abbreviations like 'u' or 'soz' or 'prolly' in any formal learning exercise, just as we would discourage spoken slang in written work, we could consider some artefacts of speech created in the realm of electronic communication, exclamations like 'lol' and 'meh' and 'w00t', legitimate in certain prescribed contexts. The use of emoticons, moreover, might be positively encouraged as a way of achieving nuance in text based communication. Such things make the difference between learning technologies being a means of merely producing text and realising their potential as a dynamic medium for interaction and communication.

Put very simply there is a fine balance to strike between the need to set new standards for the uses of technology that are appropriate for the classroom and the need to use the technology in ways and for purposes that children recognise and find stimulating and engaging. Obviously these two considerations are not opposed in principle; children quickly adapt to standards of conduct and behaviour in the classroom – in relation to play, for example, and do not find this environment antithetical to stimulating activity. The problem is that the computer creates an additional dimension to this environment and this creates new considerations that the teacher needs to address.

One obstacle to this, as noted in the last chapter, is the fact that teachers are not always confident about their own skills and lack understanding of this new dimension, which seems to open a window on a world that is more difficult for the teacher to govern and control than the confines of the physical classroom. We need to acknowledge the challenges involved in acclimatising to a learning environment that incorporates technology and training has not kept pace with investment in computers and related equipment, let alone with the pace of development in online tools. Books like this one try to address this side of the issue, by exploring definitions and suggesting applications. However, it is also necessary to try and see the internet in a broader context and one way of doing this is to try and look at the broader relevance of the internet in children's lives, not just now but in the future too.

Present and future needs

If the experiences and expectations of primary school aged children are an issue, their present and future needs are equally important. Of course, determining children's future needs is a thorny question, but – given much of what we have already said about their impact on culture and society – we should consider the internet and related technologies to be significant factors. The internet plays an important part in many spheres of social and cultural life. It supports effective communication within familial and social networks that are increasingly fragmented within a more mobile and globalised society. It promotes awareness of and participation in social and cultural events and enables new patterns of engagement with political processes. It supports new forms of economic transactions, giving access to preferential levels of service and considerable savings over more traditional forms of 'shopping'.

An ability to participate fully within modern society, then, already involves the ability to operate effectively within an online environment. This ability depends upon mastering a number of skills, which might be equated to the concept of literacy. Traditionally literacy has been defined as the ability to 'understand, interpret, create, communicate, compute and use' written or printed text, but it is a relatively small step to start applying these same skills to the realm of electronic documents and communication. Even though the internet uses the written word very heavily we need to consider how the electronic environment itself, with its use of multiple media and hypertext, changes the demands on the reader, viewer or listener, when it comes to decoding, interpreting, understanding and creating (Kress and Leeuwen 2000). In addition to this we need to consider the particular challenges presented by the way that information is stored, accessed and distributed on and across the internet. People need to know how to find information, download or play, publish and disseminate it as well.

It is worth considering these issues in a little more detail. The World Wide Web is littered with symbols and icons representing signposts and controls, which allow users to find, access and interact with information. These vary between contexts, but conform to some basic conventions that can be recognised by the user. There are a huge number of these visual cues, any one of which can help the experienced web surfer to immediately orient themselves, determine on subsequent actions or diagnose a problem. They can equally disorient and confuse the inexperienced browser. Learning to recognise and interpret these icons is an important aspect of digital literacy and yet we have not yet even started to consider how the user of the internet starts to interpret or understand a document, let alone create one. We are, in fact, only starting to scratch the surface of the symbolic lexicon that he or she needs to grasp just to comprehend the environment within which those documents are stored.

The internet itself is a medium in the sense that McLuhan (1964) described media. It is a means by which information is conveyed, but it is also meaningful in and of itself. Put another way, the internet is a literate environment in the sense that it contains many layers of coded information that draw on a learnt symbolic language and requires continual interpretation. It is also an active medium in the sense that it interacts with and affects all aspects of the ways in which information is created, interpreted and produced.

The dynamic nature of the internet is largely due to the very many different ways in which the environment can be customised. Every site and every page can be made to look and work in different ways according to the preferences or needs of the users. However, it is also due to the ways in which users interact with each other and with the content that they find 'online'. This interaction can take many forms. At one level merely visiting a site has a certain impact, as your presence is recorded and affects – albeit only very slightly – the status of site as regards search engines and usage statistics. At another level, users often have the opportunity to rate content or comment or upload 'responses' that parody or develop themes evoked by the original author. YouTube provides a good example of this. At another level of engagement, users can edit and extend content or even add their own. Put starkly, sites are created for specific audiences and the audience helps to shape that site.

The immediate, ever-present and intimate relationship between author, environment, content and audience, means that in addition to being literate and dynamic the internet is also a cultural space. Interestingly, it is not just a place that reflects cultural and sub-cultural influences, but serves as a place where cultural identities form. Internet users who engage in a shared experience around a site or a particular type of site forge new lines of communication, learn to recognise and share a distinct symbolic repertoire and even adopt quirks of language or codes exclusive to themselves. Just as we talk of the culture of the playground, where individuals acquire acceptance and status according to distinct rules and values, internet communities form cultures of their own.

What is more, in the same way that certain cultural influences – in the form of TV programmes, games or commodities like marbles and trading cards – become a sort of currency in the playground, so the internet creates and celebrates its own cultural artefacts, in the shape of multimedia creations. Crucially, just as it is easy for the outsider to miss or undervalue the significance of these social transactions in the playground, so the true cultural meaning of the things that happen online can be easily dismissed. It is easy to do so, because it is often not the intrinsic value of the commodity that is at stake but the meaning with which it is invested. Consider YouTube and the prominence enjoyed by the film itself: large in proportion to everything else on the screen, top left, bold in black against a white background. This is what the casual user always focuses on. This appears to be the sole cultural commodity being traded. However, for the fan of YouTube, the comments and the ratings on those comments are not the small change of this cultural transaction, but its absolutely highest denomination.

Now as this discussion has progressed we have focused more and more on the recreational and personal aspects of the World Wide Web. However, the internet encompasses many different contexts, each one actively oriented to a different domain or realm of activity. To return to the aspects of internet use highlighted earlier in this discussion, those opportunities that we identified for social, cultural, political and economic expression require the user to move confidently between realms. This requires a broadly literate understanding of how the internet works and an appreciation of its fundamentally dynamic character, including a facility with all the means for communication that it provides. However, it also requires the user to recognise and to be able to operate effectively within different cultural milieus, adopting appropriate patterns of speech, projecting an appropriate demeanour and conducting oneself in an appropriate way, as well as recognising all the cultural cues and symbols that allow the user to operate appropriately and confidently within that context.

In recent years the needs of children as potential users of the internet have tended to focus on their safety. However, this discussion would suggest that there are far wider issues at stake. While children are potentially vulnerable and their safety is of great importance, too great a focus on safety, particularly if this results in a retreat from the internet as a learning environment, can actually serve to make children less safe online in the longer term (Frechette 2002: xvi–xvii). In her report on children and new technologies Byron (2008) explores how we might engage children in new technologies safely by evoking an analogy with the hazards presented by motor vehicles. We teach children to navigate their environment safely by confronting those dangers, not by isolating them. Ultimately we do so because this ability to cross roads and later drive on them opens new horizons and opportunities for the next generation (Byron 2008: 39).

As we have seen, the internet offers similar opportunities providing children are taught to use it responsibly.

Of course we are entitled to ask whether these skills need to be taught. Might children not learn them in their own time? As we stated at the beginning of this chapter, not all children have equal access to technology at home. This alone provides an argument for addressing issues of digital literacy in schools. The importance of the internet as a realm of expression and a means of participation is significant and one must assume that it is going to increase in importance as time goes on. In addition to this, while we have looked at digital literacy for its distinctive features, it is important not to lose sight of the fact that it is really just a subset of the broader realm of literacy. The fact that many children are already using the literate environment that is the World Wide Web for social interaction and communication should be seen as an opportunity. The fact that they may be doing so in ways that are narrow in focus, unsuited to formal contexts like education and potentially damaging to their potential as learners, should make that sense of opportunity into one of urgent obligation.

As we have seen the ability to use the internet effectively requires more than just skills, it requires children to view and apply those skills in a reflective way. This is where formal education can connect with the informal learning that children negotiate for themselves in other contexts. Users of the internet need to be able to apply a range of skills self-consciously and in adaptable ways, reflecting the different contexts that they encounter and which they need to be able to identify, recognise and comprehend. The importance of being sensitive to context bears on the ability of the user to become an efficient and discriminating user of information and allows them to interact, communicate and collaborate with other internet users in safe, constructive and rewarding ways.

The web requires the world of formal education to look critically at itself and to consider whether the skills of teachers and the traditional view of the learning environment are relevant in a fast changing social, cultural and economic world. However, the key features of the way the web works and the requirements it makes of users mean that many of the traditional values of formal education are as, if not more, relevant to the online realm as they are in the embodied world. This is particularly clear, given the need to develop critical, analytical and reflective skills. At what point do we need to start developing skills of this sort? A combination of the two factors considered in this chapter so far, the expectations and experiences of children on one hand and their future needs on the other, would suggest that primary school is not too early.

The pedagogy

This, then, leads us to consider the third way in which we might seek to construct a rationale for the use of Web 2.0 technologies: the ways in which they operate constructively alongside the established practices, values and objectives associated with formal education.

Although computers have not transformed the educational environment as some anticipated, they are now indisputably part of the fabric of almost every school. What is more, they are embedded in the curriculum and form a key strand within national strategies relating to education. This has been the situation for about 20 years and in this time it was assumed that computers and internet technology would have an impact on pedagogy. More specifically there has been a distinct expectation that new pedagogies would emerge, reflecting the integration of computers and internet technology into the values and practices of the school.

A number of new approaches to learning have indeed been vaunted. Computers have been associated with radical visions of a future in which all learning is mediated electronically, dispensing with the inequalities and with the constraints of time and physical location that characterise the modern, western system of education. In recent times, with the advent of the World Wide Web, interest has started to coalesce around the democratising influence of the internet, for its potential to empower learners, both in terms of their relationship to the teacher and to the whole notion of knowledge acquisition and creation.

For Papert (1980), uses of technology that promote rote learning were limited and he sought a solution in devising strategies according to which children taught the computer. He developed a computer language called logo that enabled children to programme a robot or 'turtle' in ways that developed problem solving and mathematical skills. Most importantly he sought an approach to learning that focused on the individual creativity of the child and, following Piaget's position, favoured a pupil-led process of knowledge construction (ibid.: 30–2).

Adopting a more explicit focus on internet technology, Anderson devised a pedagogy founded upon the dual principles of knowledge-centred and interaction-based learning (Anderson 2004). According to his approach, learning could be supported by the fund of information available on the World Wide Web and, specifically, by features like hyper-linking that promoted independent discovery and enquiry based activities. In this model the teacher acquired the role of guide and mediator, helping to shape the learning process through questioning and formative assessment. However, for Anderson, the learning community and collaboration within it and with wider communities of practice was the key driver for learning (ibid.: 49).

Both of these theories are heavily influenced by wider pedagogic debates. Papert was heavily and avowedly influenced by Piaget, while Anderson, with his emphasis on learning communities, owed much to theorists like Vygotsky and Wenger. The essential core of these 'new' pedagogies is ultimately a restatement of constructivist principles that have resided at the heart of the pedagogical debate for more than half a century. However, with the development of Web 2.0 technologies, aspects of this debate have acquired new momentum. In the next few paragraphs we will examine why this might be the case. What opportunities do new internet technologies bring for engaging with wider pedagogical debates and to what extent do they create new opportunities for learning and teaching?

One very obvious characteristic of the internet is that it provides users with much freer access to information. From its conception the internet was intended to support the sharing of knowledge and many young people are already familiar with the idea of the internet as an information space; a place where they can find things out. Of course there have always been information spaces: libraries, bookshelves, forums like the dinner table – where children might encounter trusted, well informed people who can answer questions. However, the internet provides a slightly different kind of information space, partly due to the environment it provides and partly because of the situation of the individual when using it.

The issue of the wider environment is an important one. It is summed up nicely by those who provide internet services and claim that we can use them, 'from the comfort of our own homes'. The appeal of this might be measured according to the popularity of online supermarket shopping, or the volume of booking services that are now conducted, quite routinely, on the World Wide Web. Why make a special journey to a train station or spend potentially costly minutes waiting in a queue on the day of travel, when one can access more reliable timetable information and even cheaper tickets online? While this can be easily overstated, the internet has brought about a shift in power. We, as consumers of information, are no longer reliant on a single source and can make lots of related investigations that relate to our own needs. For example, we might quickly compare costs involved in alternative means of transport or check the weather or the availability of accommodation at our destination.

Of course formal learning is school based, and we are not yet at the stage where children can engage from the 'comfort of their own home'. Apart from anything else we would not want them to lose out on the opportunities for direct and immediate interaction with teachers and other children afforded by talk and play in a classroom environment. However, these examples serve to illustrate a fundamental shift in the way in which we – children included – encounter information. Where we used to rely on established and recognised institutions in order to mediate our access to information, we are now much more independent. Translated into the arena of school and formal education, the internet is seen to herald a shift from a world in which the children are 'fed' information to one in which they 'fish' for themselves (Papert 1993). By feeding we mean that schools pre-select and package information according to preconceived ideas about what children need to know. The notion of fishing on the other hand encapsulates the idea that children should be able to decide what they need to know, or should at least be partners in that process (Wenger 2004: 267).

The situation of the users in relation to the internet is also an important consideration. Internet users are, from the perspective of other users at least, anonymous. Children are therefore able to function more independently of labels that might attach to their gender, ethnic background, and physical appearance and so on. Identity is also less fixed and so the internet can feel like a more fluid social environment, where one is less constrained by other people's beliefs about you as an individual. As Garner and Gillingham put it, 'The internet is not so hierarchical, so attentive to physical shortcomings and social status as, for instance, most high schools that we know' (Garner and Gillingham 1996: 16). It is also true that age itself is less of a barrier to accessing information than it often is in other realms.

Even on the physical level the internet is a place without high shelves and although a considerable amount of content might be put out of reach by other means, placed behind subscription-only portals for example, this is not obvious to the everyday user, who can normally get something on any subject via Wikipedia or a common search engine. At the same time, while many areas of the internet are out of bounds to children, being age restricted or banned by local child safety settings, the internet feels like a safe environment with few of the immediate physical dangers, such as traffic, or social pressures, like 'bigger kids'.

Of course these same characteristics of the internet, the essential anonymity of the individual user and the accessibility of materials and resources, provide the context for many of the dangers of the environment. These dangers include predatory activities by adults, bullying by other children and exposure to inappropriate materials. However, as

Byron observes in her review on children and new technology, 'potential risks online are closely correlated with potential benefits' (Byron 2008: 21). The anonymity and freedom of movement provided by the internet offers an opportunity to create what Parker describes as the 'space that invites the voice of the individual and the voice of the group' (Parker 1998: 73).

Clearly any exploration of the pedagogy behind the use of the internet and the online environment must explore this notion of learner voice. Again, it is important to acknowledge that we are invoking theories that do not derive from or assume any engagement with technology or internet mediated forms of communication. An appreciation of the importance of the voice of the learner has long been recognised. Vygotsky developed ideas around the relationship between learning and social interaction, ideas that found expression in his notion of a 'zone of proximal development' (Daniels 2001). This 'zone' was the difference or measure of possible learning that separated what a learner could do on their own and what was possible through collaboration with a more experienced 'teacher'. Despite the importance of the role of the teacher, however, Vygotsky's theory was distinguished by the concept of collaboration and the central and active role played by the learner themselves (Vygotsky 1978: 86).

This concept acquires a more emphatic form, in Bakhtin's discussion of 'dialogics', in which all cultural and social expressions are seen to exist in response to or in anticipation of others (Bakhtin 1981). For Bakhtin identity, learning, meaning and knowledge existed only in the context of dialogue. Dialogics as a tool for learning has acquired considerable momentum in recent years, drawing on the works of educationalists, like Bruner and developments in psychology and neuroscience. As described by Alexander, dialogic teaching becomes: 'an approach to teaching which in a highly disciplined fashion harnesses the power of talk to stimulate and extend pupils' thinking and advance their learning and understanding' (Alexander 2004).

Speaking more generally, we are firmly located in the social constructivist way of thinking and should look for fruitful interaction between this theoretical construct and the use of the internet and related tools. The link between social interaction and the idea of dialogue as a means of constructing meaning and knowledge force us to consider the distinction between learning and teaching, which is just one means by which learning might be achieved (Wenger 2004: 225). Talk and social interaction are not restricted to the school environment after all. In fact one could argue that didactic approaches to teaching mean that opportunities for talk and social interaction are limited in the classroom. As we have seen, the online environment allows teachers to confront and engage with numerous informal patterns of learning and interaction. We have also seen that commentators have seen the internet as a place where learners can express themselves freely and in new relationships with each other and with the teacher. In the second section of this book we explore tangible way in which web tools can support meaningful opportunities for social interacion and dialogue. However, before we lose our focus on the connections between internet tools and pedagogy it is important to move from a general discussion about the internet to a more specific exploration of the relationship between pedagogy and Web 2.0. In doing so two particular viewpoints emerging from the constructivist paradigm are of particular importance. The first is summarised by Wenger, who talks about learning as being a question of active participation 'in the practices of social communities and constructing identities in relation to these communities' (2004: 40) and a process that 'belongs to the realm of practice and experience' (ibid.: 225). The second viewpoint is one that seeks to move from preconceived learning objectives and cover-all approaches to assessment, to a focus on individual pupils that seeks not to highlight deficits in their knowledge, but rather emphasises creativity and independence. This is captured nicely by Bernstein who speaks about this distinction in terms of performance and competency based approaches to learning (Bernstein 2000).

These themes provide a useful arena in which to consider the potential of social software as it provides ready access to communities in the world outside the classroom and, in many cases, tools that the teacher can use to mediate and control interaction. These tools are also a means to engage children's creativity and provide an arena in which they can explore new roles and new ideas in relative safety. We have already seen ways in which this can happen and develop these ideas much further in the second section of this book.

Those readers who are familiar with literature on learning theories may have wondered why this discussion has not evoked Downes or Prenski and their notions of learning 2.0. As the name suggests learning 2.0 is an approach to learning that embraces the principle of Web 2.0. It is founded on a radical interpretation of the impact of the web and specifically on Web 2.0 tools, whereby a 'medium, in which information was transmitted and consumed, into being a platform, in which content is created, shared, remixed, repurposed and passed along' (Downes 2005). This theory has not been raised until now because it is predicated on the belief that the development of new web tools has run alongside a similar shift in the mentality of learners. Where opponents of the web see the internet as causing surface learning and short attention spans, Downes heralds this as the dawn of new critical skills, an era in which learners are able to multi-task and are capable of rapid information processing. If they appear to fall short of the standards expected in school this is due to the inflexibility of those standards and the inability of schools to reflect social and cultural realities.

To an extent, the importance of the learning theory that resides at the heart of this approach, removes it from the scope of the present discussion. The concept of the 'digital native' as Prenski coined it, is an interesting lens through which to look at the learner, but provides only a tentative basis on which to construct new roles for learners and teachers (Bennett *et al.* 2008). However, no discussion of learning technology is complete without a closer look at learning 2.0 and, interestingly it resides firmly, within the constructivist framework identified in the works of Wenger and Bernstein (Jaffer 2009: 14). Of particular interest is the ways in which learning 2.0 makes explicit many of the ways in which the internet supports the development of learning communities and for giving the learner independence and creative freedom.

In this book we do not go as far as Downes and Prenski, in attempting to see the development of web technologies in the context of a wider transformation of learning styles. However we shall go on to look at many of the ways in which Web 2.0 tools create opportunities for children to engage with questions. It focuses on the independence that Web 2.0 affords children in shaping their own learning experience and on the ways in which related tools allow them to apply creative skills in expressing and articulating the knowledge that they acquire. It identifies the inherently collaborative and social nature of the web, exploring how individuals can come to engage with the essential provisionality of knowledge through participation in learning communities and explore a number of different roles, including critic, author and publisher, as part of the process.

Chapter 4

Web 2.0 and the primary curriculum

This section of the book seeks to explore and review the place of Web 2.0 within the curriculum and will do the following:

- how new Web 2.0 tools might complement the curriculum;
- investigate some of the proposed changes to the curriculum in relation to new technologies;
- consider how ICT and new technologies can be connected to some current government initiatives;
- examine the agenda for the personalisation of learning;
- seek to explore the place of new technologies in relation to personalisation.

ICT and the National Curriculum

This chapter does not set out to justify the place of technology within the National Curriculum (DFEE and QCA 1999); this has already been written about extensively. What this chapter will seek to achieve is to review the changing fortunes of ICT in the National Curriculum (DFEE and QCA 1999). Additionally, it will consider the relationship between these statutory documents and the new internet tools discussed in this book.

When the National Curriculum (DFEE and QCA 1999) acquired its current form it established Information and Communication Technology (ICT) as a foundation subject and assured its place as a focused area of study. Links to ICT were also written into every other curriculum subject's programme of study (DFEE and QCA 1999), thereby giving this subject further prominence. The election of the New Labour government in 1997 saw this curriculum area acquire more status. Educational change was one of the themes at the heart of New Labour's manifesto and technology was an integral part of this. Emphasis was placed on creating a 'knowledge based society equipped with the accompanying appropriate skills; the use of ICT in education was seen as central to this process and would "upskill" the future workforce ensuring its employability' (Buckingham: 2007). Technology, and its use, was also linked to the ongoing objective of raising 'standards', with educational ministers persuading voters that technology could be part of the answer. For example, in 2003 Charles Clarke spoke of the impact technology had on pupil performance (Buckingham 2007). New initiatives also realised the increasing influence of technology within the educational arena.

The National Grid for Learning established in 1998 was set up to help schools improve their use of ICT and, in 2003/4, the DCSF Primary Schools Whiteboard Expansion Project provided funding to 21 local educational authorities to help them purchase interactive whiteboards for the primary classroom. Meanwhile, the Primary National Strategy's Literacy and Numeracy Frameworks had ICT interwoven throughout their programmes, and this process has continued and developed up until the present day (DFE 2011).

Also in 1998, the QCA established widely used schemes of work that embedded ICT throughout the curriculum and government quangos and think-tanks were established to help embed the use of ICT in school. For example, BECTA (British Educational Communications and Technology Agency) was established in order to conduct and evaluate research in this area and Futurelab (a technology research laboratory) has acquired an influential place in educational circles, promoting innovative ways to use technology.

Much, therefore, has been carried out in order to establish technology at the heart of the agenda in schools. The varying and numerous initiatives, of which only a very small number have been mentioned above, can be seen to create a link between technology and primary education. However, having done so, they have also needed to reflect and address the accelerating rate of change in both fields.

Trends in education and curriculum initiatives come and go and can quickly appear dated. This is particularly true where technology plays an important part. Many of these initiatives, which have been costly for schools, have been quickly superseded by new ones that use more sophisticated technologies or new and better approaches to learning. What is more, although they have all left their mark upon the curriculum, the core curriculum documents themselves have not always been updated to reflect changing expectations. This can present a conundrum for schools, for there is a tension in trying to deliver current modes of teaching and learning when working from statutory curriculum documents that could be considered dated in relation to technology. Indeed, the view that a new form of primary curriculum is needed has been the subject of intense scrutiny over the last three years and the current state of our 'new' curriculum will be considered later on in this chapter.

Of course, the most urgent question in this book concerns the extent to which the suggestions for ICT use in current curriculum documents are relevant or inclusive of new technologies like Web 2.0 tools. At first glance, the curriculum documents, particularly the exemplars suggested for modes of work for ICT, do indeed show signs of being dated in the light of newly available learning technologies. Examined more carefully, however, the curriculum documents convey principles and expectations that resonate well with modern pedagogies and need considering.

One good aspect of the primary ICT curriculum is the deliberately generic nature of the vocabulary used about higher order thinking skills and the role of ICT in developing them. This needs to be deconstructed and examined in detail, in order to ensure that it is fully understood. Most importantly, the Programme of Study (DFEE and QCA 1999) for ICT encourages the development of what is often called 'ICT capability', although the term is not explicitly used in the document itself.

ICT capability

The ICT Programme of Study (DFEE and QCA 1999) requires children to combine technological skills and routines in order to develop their ability to use ICT to achieve wider learning outcomes, which is the essence of 'capability'. Prospective teachers need to understand the difference between what can be called 'routine operations' and activities that require 'capability', for if teachers only use the former in their use of ICT within the curriculum their lessons are likely to lack more effective learning scenarios.

A technique, or routine, is a skill that children have to learn when using technology. An example of a technique that children have to learn could be how to send or how to add an attachment to an email. To children these techniques might initially prove fairly tricky, but, as they become more familiar with the email software they are using, the task of sending emails would gradually become automatic and provide little challenge. Children do need to learn ICT skills and routines, but this sort of activity must not constitute the only source of ICT work that they encounter.

Capability, on the other hand, combines skills and routines that allow children to solve a problem or carry out a task. This requires much more rigour, understanding and application of knowledge and should be the desired sort of learning carried out during ICT lessons. Kennewell *et al.* (2000) suggests that ICT capability is formulated from five separate components:

- routines – knowing how to use the tools;
- techniques – understanding effective applications and strategies for their use;
- concepts – recognising intellectual and theoretical rationales for applications;
- processes – comprehending the place of ICT in broader learning activities;
- higher order skills – developing critical and reflective faculties as a result.

It is probable that when children are exhibiting 'capability' in their work they are most likely using ICT purposefully, to enhance another curriculum area and this is the essence of good ICT use. ICT should be used as a problem solving tool across the curriculum to tackle tasks that have relevance and context to a child. The child should use their 'capability' in order to do this and here we come to understand the significance of the term. Learning ICT outside the broader context provided by capability has limited relevance. ICT tools change very rapidly and learning how to use them for their own sake bears little resemblance to how technology is used in real life.

The ICT Programme of Study (DFEE and QCA 1999) is concerned very much with 'capability' and the flexibility of Web 2.0 tools, their accessibility and their potential to promote collaborative, creative activities, means that they provide an ideal context for activities of this sort. It could be suggested that Web 2.0 tools are also concerned with this same phenomenon and this gives them absolute relevance to our current curriculum. For instance, learning how to create a blog might be called a 'routine' skill that children have to acquire. However, maintaining and formatting a blog to include various different types of visual media requires the child to demonstrate a combination of skills, understanding and knowledge. What is more, using a blog format to write a diary over a number of weeks would not only reveal much capability, but also constitutes a purposeful, cross-curricular application of technology in the context of a meaningful task and provides a powerful learning experience as a result.

So many Web 2.0 tools require children to use a combination of routines in their application and this provides a very meaningful reason for their inclusion in the school's curriculum. The term 'capability' should be remembered and considered when reading some of the suggested exemplars of use of Web 2.0 tools that are discussed further on in the book.

Knowledge, skills and understanding

Finding things out

1 Pupils should be taught:

- to talk about what information they need and how they can find and use it (for example: searching the internet or a CD-ROM; using printed material or asking people);
- how to prepare information for development using ICT, including selecting suitable sources, finding information, classifying it and checking it for accuracy (for example: finding information from books or newspapers; creating a class database; classifying by characteristics and purposes and checking that the spelling of names is consistent);
- to interpret information, to check it is relevant and reasonable and to think about what might happen if there were any errors or omissions.

Developing ideas and making things happen

2 Pupils should be taught:

- how to develop and refine ideas by bringing together, organising and reorganising text, tables, images and sound as appropriate (for example, desktop publishing or multimedia presentations);
- how to create, test, improve and refine sequences of instructions to make things happen and to monitor events and respond to them (for example: monitoring changes in temperature, detecting light levels and turning on a light);
- to use simulations and explore models in order to answer 'What if ... ?' questions, to investigate and evaluate the effect of changing values and to identify patterns and relationships (for example: simulation software and spreadsheet models).

Exchanging and sharing information

3 Pupils should be taught:

- how to share and exchange information in a variety of forms, including e-mail (for example: displays, posters, animations and musical compositions);
- to be sensitive to the needs of the audience and think carefully about the content and quality when communicating information (for example: work for presentation to other pupils, writing for parents and publishing on the internet).

Reviewing, modifying and evaluating work as it progresses

4   Pupils should be taught to:

- review what they and others have done to help them develop their ideas;
- describe and talk about the effectiveness of their work with ICT, comparing it with other methods and considering the effect it has on others (for example: the impact made by a desktop-published newsletter or poster);
- talk about how they could improve future work.

Breadth of study

5   During the key stage, pupils should be taught the knowledge, skills and understanding through:

- working with a range of information to consider its characteristics and purposes (for example: collecting factual data from the internet and a class survey to compare the findings);
- working with others to explore a variety of information sources and ICT tools (for example: searching the internet for information about a different part of the world, designing textile patterns using graphics software, using ICT tools to capture and change sounds);
- investigating and comparing the uses of ICT inside and outside school.

(DFEE and QCA 1999)

ICT and creativity

One theme that has become prominent in curricular initiatives is that of ICT's link to creativity. Creativity across the whole curriculum has been a dominant theme in schools and is associated with good learning environments. The National Curriculum (DFEE and QCA 1999) states that:

> By providing rich and varied contexts for pupils to acquire, develop and apply a broad range of knowledge, understanding and skills, the curriculum should enable pupils to think creatively and critically, to solve problems and to make a difference for the better. It should give them the opportunity to become creative, innovative, enterprising and capable of leadership to equip them for their future lives as workers and citizens.

(DFEE and QCA 1999: 11–12)

The importance of creativity as an essential ingredient to success was also reinforced by the document 'Excellence and Enjoyment' (DfES 2003a). One need only skim the document to encounter the term 'creativity'. Indeed, it occurs in the executive summary, as a feature associated with the best primary schools in England. This theme continues throughout the document as creative teaching is said to:

- improve pupils' self-esteem, motivation and achievement;
- develop skills for adult life;
- develop the talent of the individual.

Facer and Williamson (2004) summarise well the rising status of this concept by arguing that:

> Creativity is no longer regarded as a discrete skill required for art, drama or music, but rather it is seen as central to children's abilities to work imaginatively and with a purpose, to judge the value of their own contributions and those of others, and to fashion critical responses to problems across all subjects in the curriculum.
>
> (Facer and Williamson 2004: 5)

Several publications have recognised the potential of ICT to promote creativity. In fact both these aspects of the curriculum could be seen to complement each other well, given their cross-curricular applications. The National Curriculum Online (QCDA) makes a link to the importance of understanding technology and creativity by stating that 'pupils who are creative will be prepared for a rapidly changing world', while Bennett and McBurnie (2005) note that elements of ICT can bring enormous benefits to all aspects of the creative curriculum, particularly in the context of problem solving scenarios.

Condie *et al.* (2007) also note the potential for ICT in helping to deliver a creative curriculum. They observe that the quality of the work produced depends not only on a teacher's understanding and application of hardware, but also on a working knowledge of pedagogy and meta-cognition, which ensures that higher order thinking skills are accessed by children. BECTA (2008a) argue that in a classroom that is conducive to creativity, ICT can be purposefully used by pupils to express their ideas, to respond to tasks in unpredictable ways, to use a combination of intuition, logic, reason and spontaneity, to make connections between classroom work and outside experiences and to experiment and take risks. Certainly, once a practitioner has a good understanding of good learning scenarios it quickly becomes possible to think of a whole range of applications for ICT that provoke creative and imaginative responses in children across the whole primary age range.

Examples could include:

- The use of peripheral toy devices that use technology to create a range of creative responses in young children. The use of objects like metal detectors and walkie-talkies, as well as a variety of ICT based toys like cash tills, cash dispensers, mobile phones and cameras. These can induce a variety of play based responses, which encourage imagination and creativity and are a far cry from more traditional views of children sitting alone at a computer making limited responses to a piece of curriculum related software.
- Children using simple programming languages to control robots to access higher level thinking skills through trial and error, predicting, learning from mistakes, hypothesising, sequencing and making connections.
- The advent of technological tools that give pupils the ability to respond to learning tasks in a visually literate way has paved the way for more creative responses to producing work as opposed to merely hard copy, text based assignments. For instance, the use of software that allows children to work with animation or the use of video cameras to record thoughts allow children to produce work that could show a more 'creative' and colourful product that may have been unobtainable for many children when they were just using the written word to express themselves.

Table 4.1 Features of Web 2.0 promoting creativity. Adapted from Loveless NACCE framework for creativity (2012: 12)

Features of ICT	NACCE framework for creativity	Features of Web 2.0
Provisionality (to make changes)	Using imagination	Ethos of enquiry
Interactivity (engagement, feedback)	A fashioning process	Participation – collaboration- peer assessment
Capacity	Pursuing purpose	Self-managers – motivation
Range and Speed	Being original	Ownership
Automatic functions (storing, transferring, displaying and interrogating information)	Judging value	Reflective learning/critical thinking

The visual literacy strand can be reinforced and extended by the use of Web 2.0 tools. As we have seen the core technologies that underpin social software support the creation of diverse applications and new tools are emerging all the time. These allow pupils to produce creative learning products, which can now be immediately shared and responded to, not only within the class based community of learners, but with the outside community both locally and globally. Examples of these tools and suggested applications are raised in the second section of this book.

Loveless (2012: 12) discusses the theme of creativity further, noting that 'a characteristic of creativity with digital technologies would be the recognition of the potential of the features of ICT to be exploited and experimented with to support creative processes'. It could be argued that Web 2.0 tools now extend methods for creative responses across the curriculum and this gives them a vital place within the school curriculum today. Indeed, at the very heart of Web 2.0 is the principle that users 'add value', for Web 2.0 depends on their adding content and this imbues it with a creative dimension.

Interestingly, Loveless compares the vocabulary associated with creativity used by the National Advisory Committee on Creative and Cultural Education (NACCE 1999) with the unique characteristics offered by ICT. The table created by Loveless has been reproduced above, with additional column listing characteristics associated with Web 2.0. This helps to give an insight into the similarities between features associated with creativity and some of the processes associated with social software.

Proposed changes to the curriculum

At the time of writing this text, the curriculum is in a state of flux and there is much uncertainty as to the look and direction of primary education. With the change of government in May 2010, education has become subject to scrutiny with a new ministerial education team who are promising a review of the curriculum. However, as yet, the finer detail of this has not been decided. Before the 2010 general election the primary curriculum had been subject to particular inspection and had just undergone a series of reviews that were initiated by teacher dissatisfaction with the current 'over-prescribed' curriculum.

The Cambridge Review (Alexander and Flutter 2009) and the Rose Report (DCSF 2009) discussed the challenges faced by primary education and proposed new versions of the curriculum. The changes detailed by Rose (DCSF 2009), were favoured by the Labour government and set to inform changes to the curriculum. Ultimately, it was not sanctioned by parliament before the national elections and the new government have not continued with Rose's suggestions. Instead they have now declared an impending rewrite of the curriculum from their viewpoint. Nevertheless, much of what he suggested was the result of careful research, and, for this reason alone his ideas must be seen as being worthy of consideration. While some of what Rose suggested will be ignored it is likely that many themes, particularly those relating to personalised learning, may still be realised in the future (DCSF 2009).

Rose's Final Independent Review of the Primary Curriculum (DCSF 2009) embraced the role of technology, placing it firmly centre stage. The status of technology was raised and prioritised by naming Information and Communication Technology (ICT) as a core curriculum requirement and one of the 'essentials for learning and life' (2009: 11). He suggested that ICT should be taught both discretely and embedded across the curriculum, reflecting its general importance within society and day to day life. The emerging potential of Web 2.0 as a future educational tool, in particular, was acknowledged.

Rose stated that children should have a sound grasp of ICT and that this was fundamental to their engagement with society (DCSF 2009: 15). He also advocated that children should have the ICT skills that would enable them to apply the technology of the future. The report discussed the importance of recognising the increasing digitisation of information worldwide and of reflecting this in the primary curriculum, requiring children to be fully digitally literate. This would involve children learning to use and apply a range of ICT tools including Web 2.0 applications.

Rose (DCSF 2009) suggests that to ignore this would be to produce a generation of children divided into ICT 'haves' and 'have-nots'. He felt that this situation would pose a considerable threat to both economic well being and social cohesion (DCSF 2009: 70). It could be suggested that the report also encourages us to infer the potential of Web 2.0 by using phrases associated with the principles of social software like 'participation' and the understanding of digital literacy to 'deepen cognitive skills' (ibid.). These ideas were stated more directly in BECTA's *Contribution to the Rose Review* (2009), which embraces the opportunities offered by social software and was particularly clear about its potential to produce what the authors coin as the fully 'digitally literate' child.

This report comments on the importance of connectivity in association with globalisation and the subsequent economic opportunities that this might promote. It suggests that technology forms a vital part of a fully rounded modern education (BECTA 2009: 5) and asserts the importance of the participatory nature of new internet tools by stressing that children should not just be passive users of online content, but also producers of new material. The authors state that 'Learners must be both users and creators of information, using technology to develop knowledge, skills and understanding' (BECTA 2009: 6). It also notes that children must become more reflective and considered in their uses of technology, in order to become fully digitally literate and to develop cognitively. They conclude that digital literacy is a learner entitlement that must be guaranteed for all pupils (BECTA 2009: 9–10) and list the following 'essential skills':

• Find and select information from digital and online sources, making judgements about accuracy and reliability.

- Create, manipulate and process information, using technology to capture and organise data, in order to investigate patterns and trends; explore options using models and simulations and combine still and moving images, sounds and text to create multimedia products.
- Collaborate, communicate and share information using connectivity to work with and present to, people and audiences within and beyond the school.
- Refine and improve their work, making full use of the nature and pliability of digital information to explore options and improve outcomes. (BECTA 2009: 12)

The preceding paragraphs demonstrate the emerging importance of new technology in primary education. Much of what Rose (DCSF 2009) and BECTA (2009) have stated about technology and the use of Web 2.0 tools has been taken up by the media and discussed at some length. Unfortunately these discussions have been somewhat sensationalised with Web 2.0 applications being reported in a negative light. For instance David Laws, the Liberal Democrat schools spokesman, was quoted by Paton (2009) in an interview for the *Daily Telegraph* as saying:

> The curriculum must not be dumbed down as a result of these changes ... Any reform must not prioritise headline-grabbing gimmicks over the need to get the basics right. Of course it is vital that children are able to use and understand modern technology, but they must have the basic knowledge and skills enabling them to do this properly.

Cohen (2009) in an article entitled 'Exit Winston Churchill, enter Twitter', strikes a similar tone when she cites Gove who states that Rose's curriculum: 'proposes to replace solid knowledge with nods towards all the latest technological fashions'. Statements such as these give a flavour of how Rose's suggestions about Web 2.0 have been taken out of context. They demonstrate how easily views can develop around a superficial understanding of the nature of social software and how easily research can be subordinated to political agendas. Rather than advocating the uncritical adoption of popular tools Rose's recommendations could be interpreted as a long awaited acknowledgement of the need to use new forms of technology in constructive and creative ways.

At about the same time as Rose was formulating his report, Alexander was directing a parallel study entitled the Cambridge Review of the Primary Curriculum (Alexander and Flutter 2009). Published in 2009 this report constitutes a wide-ranging, independent enquiry into the state of education and the nature of childhood in the United Kingdom. The final report contains some 640 pages in 24 chapters and represents one of the most comprehensive investigations into the nature of the primary school child's experience of school life. It does not place technology so firmly in the centre of the curriculum as Rose's recommendations proposed. Instead ICT was presented as supporting activities that should be conducted across the curriculum.

Underpinning most of the research in the Cambridge Review is a belief in the importance of communication and dialogue to a child's education and ICT is presented as having an important role to play in this context. The document notes that the best teaching should enhance children's learning by promoting collaboration, challenge and purposeful talk, teaching that is 'dialogic' in nature. This is where classroom activities place debate and discussion at the heart of the learning process, seeking strategies that require collective responses and in which children act in ways that are reciprocal and mutually supportive. Such an approach is intended to create a 'learning-dynamic' that promotes critical thinking and enquiry.

Within the context of this discussion it is argued that ICT has the potential to promote oracy and literacy. Schools can, the review argues, maintain the developmental and educational primacy of talk by developing the language component of the curriculum in ways that explore the relationship between new and more traditional forms of communication. In this way Alexander and Flutter (2009) acknowledge the fundamental relationship between ICT and communication, which is so often overlooked in approaches that focus too exclusively on the mechanical processes involved in 'utilising' technology. As we have seen the notion of Web 2.0 – the social web as we have defined it – is founded on principles of participation in the form of creative expression and dialogue. In this way, therefore, we can establish one fundamental link between the principles that underpin the tools discussed in this book and those that inform curriculum design. However, the principle of participation – the emphasis on the contribution of the individual – allows us to go further and assert a link with another principle that informs much of the discussion around the curriculum at present: that is the need to personalise learning.

The concept of 'personalised learning' first emerged within the context of the 'Every Child Matters' (DfES 2003a) agenda. The 'aims and outcomes' for children as detailed in the Every Child Matters documentation (DfES 2003a) talk about the importance of acknowledging the child's view and the involvement of all children in achieving their own educational potential. The Every Child Matters (DfES 1993a) agenda attempted to address problems with educational policy at the time, which was seen to be standards driven and overly influenced by targets. The Labour government of the time sought to reform an approach that had been characterised as a 'one size fits all' solution, by re-engaging educationalists with the voice and views of the child.

The DCSF document Personalised Learning – A Practical Guide (2008a: 5) describes this type of approach as:

> ... taking a highly structured and responsive approach to each child's and young person's learning, in order that all are able to progress, achieve and participate. It means strengthening the link between learning and teaching by engaging pupils – and their parents – as partners in learning.

The pedagogy of 'personalisation' is associated with improving standards and raising attainment. It is connected to 'tailoring learning' to a child's individual needs in order that he or she might make more rapid and more meaningful progress in their learning. Personalisation is therefore seen as a more highly responsive strategy than differentiation, an approach to learning with which it is usually linked. The DCSF (2008a: 7) states that personalisation expects that all children will fulfil their early promise and develop latent potential and emphasises the importance of ensuring participation, fulfilment and success in terms of personal targets and progress plans. However, a student focus raises one problem for it is not obvious how the desire to tailor the educational experience for individual children can be managed by a single education system. The dilemma that this aspiration presents is summed up nicely by Green et al. (2005: 5) when they conclude that personalisation requires that: 'the logic of education systems should be reversed so that it is the system that conforms to the learner, rather than the learner to the system'.

For Hargreaves (2005) this dilemma is to be overcome through a focus on meta-cognition, the awareness of learning how to learn, how to monitor, evaluate, and to control thinking as a part of the broader learning process. He argues that effective learning cannot be attributed to just one strategy and that good learning environments are achieved by a 'family of learning practices' (2005: 9) within which good meta-cognitive skills make learners autonomous and intelligent and the resulting indepen-dence is key in achieving personalisation.

ICT has been said to help the personalisation of learning and an increasing number of texts and publications can be found that discuss this subject. For example, BECTA (2009: 4) states that: 'Used correctly within the education system, technology can con-tribute to supporting each learner as they develop the thinking and learning skills they will need in the future.'

In an earlier guidance document on promoting creativity with ICT BECTA (2008a) suggests that personalised learning and technology is at the centre of national aspirations for education and is widely associated with the notion that this could contribute to helping children to learn in better ways. Bennet *et al.* (2007) note that personalisa-tion is made possible via ICT as it enables learning to be tailored to the needs of indi-vidual learners and provides instant feedback based on the choices they have made. Hargreaves states that 'the curriculum and new technologies gateways are critical to personalisation because they offer potential ways in which the experience of school might become more engaging for students' (2006: 6). However, the best way to explore the ways in which Web 2.0 can help to achieve the goals of personalisation is to situate the discussion within the context of specific teaching strategies and we will follow the headings of Green *et al.* (2005) in doing this.

Choices (learner voice and choice)

Perhaps the most straightforward route to personalisation is provided by the principle of choice, giving the individual child a degree of flexibility about what and how they learn and how they demonstrate that learning. Green *et al.* (2005) note that effective choices depend upon the meaningfulness and variety of experiences that the child can draw upon and emphasise the importance of providing children with diverse experi-ences of this kind within the classroom. In developing this point, they observe that web tools are an under-used resource. Those tools that promote communication and colla-boration with other children from diverse backgrounds and distant places might be seen as having a particularly good application here. Similarly it is relevant to consider how similar tools can create opportunities for adults working in creative ways, as wri-ters or performers perhaps, or who function in other capacities that are relevant to learning in the primary classroom.

In addition to this, it is important to consider how technology can support an approach to teaching that seeks to provide children with opportunities to exert choice within the context of their learning. Here we might focus on the potential of technol-ogy to support creative expression. Choice is fundamental to creativity in that it allows, demands even, that children make decisions about a range of issues in terms of how to approach specific problems, how to represent their understanding and how to communicate a message. In this context then it is important to consider ways in which web tools provide children with opportunities to be creative and a whole chapter in the second half of this book is devoted to this theme.

Skills and knowledge (curriculum)

Like Alexander and Flutter (2009) this part of Green *et al.*'s document emphasises the importance of student dialogue and communication. However, in addition to emphasising the importance of participation, they stress the significance of technology's potential to support different forms and modes of communication and the opportunities for choice that this affords. They highlight how such tools allow students to form networks of knowledge, not just within the school, but with the outside community and the wider world. Their argument acknowledges the problem of a prescribed curriculum that often prevents children from learning in ways that suit them, in favour of learning an established set of content. Often, what children might feel motivates them, or what they are good at, is undervalued or seen as trivial, inferior forms of learning. Technologies are emphasised here in helping children and educators to collaborate and to enable the student voice to be heard.

For example, there is discussion of the use of voting systems with whiteboards at the micro level of the individual lesson, and the use of web based communication tools, such as blogs and wikis to create 'virtual democracies' and 'learning communities' at the level of the school or the community (Green *et al.* 2005). Both of these technologies provide children with a stronger voice in decision making processes relating to school and to the learning process and, again, a chapter in the second section looks specifically at opportunities to promote children emerging as effective communicators.

Learning environments (pedagogies and institutions)

This theme refers to a number of different strategies but the one that has been most fully realised in the primary arena is that of the development of the virtual learning environment (VLE) or the alternatively named learning platforms. BECTA (2008a) argues that learning platforms are one of the most important resources for personalisation, extending the learning environment in ways that give children control over when they choose to access learning resources, not just in school hours or when the teacher dictates. The platform also gives the ability for a child to work at their own pace and in an 'environment where they can be most productive' (BECTA 2008: 5).

Importantly, such platforms are said to promote the teacher's ability to work more closely with individual students, which is thought to help to improve pupil engagement even with disaffected students (BECTA 2008a: 5). BECTA (2008a) states that it is a national directive that all schools should be making full use of learning platforms by 2010 and hence this is why schools have made so much progress in this area of personalisation.

Green *et al.* (2005) expand further on the theme of VLEs and also highlight the value of virtual platforms for disaffected learners. They stress that children are not all equally equipped for learning in a traditional 'classroom' environment and that 'different people may learn better in different settings'. Excluded children and the children of traveller communities could benefit from an environment like this. The virtual learning platform can be seen to provide these children with a space in which continuity can be established, something that is missing in their encounters with school based education in the embodied world. At the same time it is easy to consider circumstances, such as periods of sickness, when a virtual learning environment could support all children.

However, Green *et al.* (2005) take the concept of personalising the learning environment a stage further than these practical considerations. They suggest that technologies may help educationalists to rethink the notion of extended schools. At present extended schools are deemed as 'functioning' by bringing more services into the school buildings and offering a variety of personal facilities to the community. A systematic discussion about the 'virtual dimension' of extended schools could, they argue, take the fulfilment of this policy to a new level. Expert services could be offered to children virtually via video conferencing, while other methods of virtual communication could offer children opportunities to make more links with businesses and organisations, both within their own community and also globally.

More generally, Green and her colleagues see uses of technology like these connecting children to the community and the wider world, thereby preventing them learning in isolation. Pedagogically speaking the technologies provide an environment which creates safe and constructive opportunities for exploration and experimentation, a theme that is developed more fully in a chapter in the next section.

Feedback (assessment and recognition)

The personalisation agenda advocates a person centred approach to assessment, as opposed to the current standardised mechanisms. Green *et al.* (2005) call for the recognition of strategies that attach value to a wider body of knowledge and exploit different forms of assessment. In doing so they advocate different uses of technology to replace the focus on text based forms of assessment. These authors state that for a true personalised system to be realised the number of ways in which learners can record their achievements must increase and that assessors must recognise that much learning is carried out outside school in order to stop an artificial separation of school based learning from society and the broader experience of private life.

This paper acknowledges the potential of technologies like mobile devices such as i-pods or picture storing systems like Flickr, as a possible vehicle for students to store records and work (Green *et al.* 2005: 26). While this is arguably more appropriate for discussions about secondary school, the ideas that these authors present are certainly worth noting, especially in their suggestion of different types of assessment for younger children to be considered and a move away 'exam based assessment of a prescribed body of knowledge'. Schools in the primary sector have a long distance to travel before assessment like this might be considered as valid. It is worth considering, however, how they might reformulate assessment to allow children to demonstrate their understanding of concepts, skills and processes and not just to show their ability to retain information.

Different learning styles and technologies are also often associated with the fulfilment of the personalisation agenda. Teachernet (2004) in the article 'What does personalised learning mean to you?' identifies engagement with the concept of learning styles as an important feature. In this context, technology can be seen to provide a means of engaging children in activities that exploit a range of learning styles and to choose approaches that suit them best. This is seen as a means of promoting greater pace within learning and a more individualised and motivating experience. All the chapters in the next section provide examples that explore the potential of technologies to create flexibility and to give students choice.

The above paragraphs make great claims for the power of technology in developing personalisation, particularly the potential of Web 2.0. Whether these claims can be turned from ideals to reality in the primary classroom remains open and Buckingham (2007), in his discussion of this issue, argues that there are indeed many 'questions to be raised' about this approach. He questions the extent to which personalisation is possible in a system that is premised on the mass delivery of public services and the relevance of the 'informal learning' that takes place in personalised learning environments, given the dominant themes in educational policy, which centre on 'high stakes' testing, a prescribed curriculum and the emphasis on 'managerialism' and accountability in school.

These considerations, he suggests, point to a 'normative' approach to learning that is antithetical to personalisation and its use by policy makers constitutes empty rhetoric or at least blind idealism. It must be admitted that many schools are yet to realise personalisation and that some of the notions detailed on the previous pages, in relation to technology, remain an aspiration. However, while we might agree that more fundamental changes are required to the dominant model of education before personalisation can be fully implemented, as a concept it remains a useful starting point for discussion on how technology can enhance learning on a more day to day basis.

Buckingham (2007) also examines the rising status of Virtual Learning Platforms in relation to the personalisation of learning. Learning platforms provide a method to fulfil the notion of learning 'any time, any place'. In addition, learning platforms can offer different ways of learning to suit a variety of different learning styles. Buckingham (2007) contrasts these positive views of VLEs with a more unexpected outcome of using this type of technology. He examines how learning platforms give parents increased access to and 'surveillance' of the work of teachers and the performance data of their children and highlights the tension that exists between these two themes.

It could be suggested that the case of learning platforms parallels the general ambivalence of the opportunities offered by technology in relation to educational policy. On the one hand new technologies are seen as a liberating and empowering mechanism, yet on the other they can also be associated with increasing control, checking and managing both the performance of the teacher and that of the student. This is a theme which is completely at odds with the liberal claims made for new uses of technology.

Despite advocating the use of ICT for personalisation, a BECTA report (Underwood 2009) has actually examined the problems of realising this approach. Underwood (2009) published a research report led by academics at Nottingham Trent University that examined some of the issues surrounding personalisation. The report states that:

> as length of service within the profession increased, positive attitudes to the value of ICT for the personalisation of learning decreased: that is, there is an inverse relationship between years of professional experience and teachers' positive perceptions of ICT for personalising learning.

> (Underwood 2009: 5)

Underwood (2009) acknowledges that the use of digital technologies does not necessarily guarantee the development of personalisation and that there existed a complex relationship between the 'e-maturity' of a school and the level of personalisation realised by their pupils. Condie *et al.* (2007) note that there is a concern that there is not yet a good understanding of how teachers can support pupils and make the most of e-learning packages in relation to personalisation. Interestingly, educationalists note (Underwood 2009: 7) the 'fractured nature of different stakeholders' in understanding of the educational concept of personalisation, thus providing further evidence of the confusion that can be associated with this notion. This research project (Underwood 2009: 7) also agrees with Buckingham's (2007) scepticism about the feasibility of personalising learning and the tension that lies between aspects of 'good learning environments' and the practicalities of a test driven curriculum. These authors argue that 'teachers felt that the personalisation of learning was constrained by the curriculum and that personalising learning was restricted in light of rather rigid assessment formats and exam pressures'.

Issues of the digital divide are also examined in relation to the personalisation of learning. Buckingham (2007) notes the potential disparity of the fulfilment of personalisation which may be more realistic for affluent children due to their increased potential of access to technology. Underwood (2009: 42) also empathises with this theme noting that 'equity of provision' could be a problem.

Caution should also be applied to the theme of ICT in fulfilling personalisation by providing facilities for different learning styles. Condie *et al.* (2007: 25) in their discussion of this area conclude that the issue of learning styles and the role of ICT in learning and teaching requires focused investigation using robust, empirical methods. They also show concern for the practicalities of identifying all pupils' cognitive style and catering for them.

Conclusion

This chapter has examined the place of Web 2.0 within the curriculum and considered its relevance. It has also discussed the possible changes to the primary curriculum and assessed how these new proposals view the nature and application of new digital tools. Web 2.0 has been considered alongside the current educational themes of creativity and personalisation. Personalisation is a vast and complex subject and the potential of the role of Web 2.0 in helping to achieve this approach has probably yet to be realised in many primary schools.

Section 2

Inspiration and ideas for teaching and learning

Preamble

In previous chapters we saw how the World Wide Web has developed software applications that allow users to exchange, share and create content in a variety of media and in a range of different contexts. We have seen how these developments have manifested in changes to the kinds of content that we encounter online and how they have led to an increase in communication, not simply to the overall volume of communication, but to the number of ways in which it is possible to communicate as well. Many of these, so called 'new' tools have direct antecedents in the technologies that have always underpinned the World Wide Web. However, the overall impact of phenomena like social networking, blogging and podcasting and the refinement of the technologies that support them have led people to talk in terms of the social web, the read write web or simply of Web 2.0.

Many of our attitudes to these technologies are informed by the ways in which they function in recreational contexts. As a result it is difficult to construct a rationale for their use in education without going through the process of redefining them for the purpose. We have attempted to do this in a variety of different ways, exploring the relevance of these technologies to, among other things, the curriculum and pedagogy. In this section we move on to explore specific applications for new web technologies in primary teaching.

An obvious approach to this task would be to address the tools that we introduced in the previous section, one at a time. However, this is problematic as it would make the discussion artificial. For one thing, teaching is complex and in order to achieve the desired learning outcomes teachers are required to use different approaches and a range of tools. For another, arranging cases studies around specific technologies would make the technology itself the context for the discussion when we really need to demonstrate how the technology can contribute within the wider context provided by specific learning and teaching scenarios. For these reasons we need to find a different way of structuring the discussion.

In the third chapter of the first section we looked at a number of different pedagogic approaches to the role of internet technology in teaching and learning. Much of this discussion focused on the ways in which technology can be used to empower the learner and to create an environment that is more focused on his or her own individual creative potential. In order to reinforce the conclusions of that chapter and in order to ensure that the learner acquires appropriate prominence in the discussion that follows, this will inform the structure of this section. Rather than chapters bearing the names of specific tools or technologies the reader will find chapters with the headings children as producers of knowledge, children as explorers and children as communicators.

Within this structure, applications for new web technologies will be proposed that frequently involve more than one tool. There will also be references to specific tools or services that do not fit neatly under the headings used so far. This is because headings like blogging and social networking are very general and embrace a large number of tools and services that have been created to work in different contexts and to produce different results. For example, among the available social bookmarking sites, we have services that allow users to create lists of links that can be annotated and shared, while others work by allowing users to place notes and annotations directly on webpages. These can then be viewed and reviewed by other users of the service. All provide a broadly similar service but do so in different ways.

At the same time, different tools have started to be combined in order to provide new results. Photo-sharing sites that once allowed visitors to search their databases with keyword searches and worked like search engines now use interactive map software to allow users to trawl maps for images of places or that were taken from geographic locations. Meanwhile interactive map services now link up to search engines and embed information about services, attractions and businesses at the locations that users select. These 'mash-ups', hybrids and variations on a theme are possible because the technologies that underpin them are not subject to patent or copyright and are therefore susceptible to endless reinvention and development.

Chapter 5

Children as producers of knowledge

This chapter provides classroom ideas and case studies that illustrate how children can realise a role as creators and producers of new knowledge, as opposed to being mere consumers of information. It covers:

- use of podcasting;
- publishing resources via media sharing sites;
- application of assessment using Web 2.0 tools;
- digital story telling.

One question that all teachers ask themselves from time to time is, 'How do I know that the children in my class are learning?' This question goes to the heart of the individual teacher's teaching philosophy and is heavily influenced by teaching style. A didactic approach can feel like a safe approach to teaching as it allows the teacher to progress at a predictable pace and to anticipate their resource requirements accurately. This is because they are the principal actor in the process and retain close control as result. In this model the teacher conveys the knowledge and often produces or at least reproduces most of the resources. If the learners realise an opportunity to produce things it is either in strictly prescribed contexts or as part of assessment.

As we saw in the last section, this is consistent with the behaviourist paradigm, according to which the purpose of education is to measure the performance of students in achieving prescribed learning outcomes and seeks to rank students according to their performance. Such an approach can be seen to be promoted by the climate created by a detailed curriculum and the difficulties presented by wide ranges of ability in the classroom. However, the problem is that it is not easy to identify and track understanding. Assessment could be seen as a measure of understanding, but even here it is possible to confuse understanding with an ability to simply reproduce knowledge.

While didactic approaches form a part of most teachers' repertoire they are normally combined with strategies that are influenced by that other great paradigm in pedagogy, constructivism. As we have seen this approach sees knowledge as being something that is created or constructed by the learner and therefore requires the learner, rather than the teacher, to be the principal actor in the process. This approach is less certain and requires the teacher to relinquish a degree of control. However, since this approach requires the learner or groups of learners to engage directly with the process of defining and creating knowledge, understanding is easier to measure. Put simply, if one can produce knowledge, then one must be said to understand the processes according to which that knowledge is constructed.

In this chapter we will look at applications and case studies that suggest ways in which new web technologies can support children's development as producers of knowledge. This is not simply a question of producing materials, the mechanical process of editing and publishing a photograph for example, but how these kinds of activity can aid in the development of understanding in the attainment of curriculum objectives. Specifically it requires us to explore how these technologies can help to stimulate and engage the creative potential of the individual child and how it can support collaborative working between children, to form communities of learners.

Classroom Idea 1: maths podcasts (recording commentaries)

In this activity a method is sought to develop understanding of fundamental mathematical principles. The example used here focuses on long multiplication, but almost any mathematical principle could be addressed in this way. This activity would follow initial teaching of the principles addressed and requires children to work in groups. Each group would be provided with a video recording of the teacher performing an example of long multiplication. The camera could be forward facing and focused on a whiteboard or mounted on a desktop tripod so that it records the teacher's working on a notepad. In either case, it is important that the numbers and operators can be seen clearly and that the teacher writes out the calculations slowly in a clear methodical way. The recording should then be published without the audio track so that the video runs with no sound. If your school uses PCs and runs the standard Windows operating system you should use the free 'Movie Maker' application as the children will need to edit the file in due course and this approach will ensure that they do not encounter compatibility problems at that stage.

The main problem that the teacher is likely to encounter at this stage is translating the video from the video camera into a format that can be loaded into movie maker. This may require you to convert the video file using the software that comes with your camera or you could simply play the video on the computer and use screen capture software like Camtasia or freeware alternatives like Cam Studio to record the video into a format like .mpg or .avi or .wmv. However, once the silent video clip has been created it can be delivered to the groups via a virtual learning environment or on disk.

The children are then set a task in which they are required to create a commentary that describes what is happening. You may feel it helpful to supply a list of terms or vocabulary that the groups are required to use at some point. This might support the groups in achieving the goal, but also ensures that all the relevant stages are addressed without providing too prescriptive a guide to the eventual outcome. In either case the groups will need time to discuss the clip and to create and rehearse a script to run alongside it. There are a couple of approaches to handling the recording of the commentary, but the simplest is probably to supply a digital voice recorder. This allows the children to start and stop the recorder easily, breaking the task of recording into more easily managed chunks. However, if no sound recorder exists then a microphone connected to a PC will provide a workable alternative, using the free 'Sound Recorder' software (Start > All Programmes > Accessories > Sound Recorder).

Once the commentary has been created it needs to be uploaded into the video editing programme that you are using, along with the video clip. It is then a relatively simple process to publish two files into a single resource. The simplest way to do this with Movie Maker is to import the video clip first. If the video was supplied to the children via a VLE, then they will need to copy the file to the computer they are using first. If it was supplied to them on disk, the disk will need to be inserted. The video should then be dragged on to the timeline or storyboard; if the bottom panel is currently displaying the storyboard it should be changed to timeline. Then import the sound file or sound files which should also be dragged, in order, to the audio track on the timeline.

The movie can then be published to the PC at which point it can be uploaded to Teacher Tube. This will require an account to be created for that website and assumes that your school allows access to this resource. The teacher can create the accounts on behalf of the students ensuring that no inappropriate information is disclosed and then pass the usernames and passwords on for the purpose. A single account will suffice for this exercise as each group can give the video a title that indicates their group name or number. In any case, the groups will need to be advised on how to title their clips so that they can be identified by a keyword search later. If it is not possible to use the Teacher Tube service a group blog will have to be created on a local virtual learning environment instead or a service like Blogger or Wordpress.

The next stage of the exercise is for the whole class to view the videos and to discuss each in turn with a view to identifying the most effective elements. Each group would then be required to excerpt the bits of their video that the class agreed were most effective and submit them to the teacher to be incorporated into a single clip.

Tool focus

TeacherTube (http://www.teachertube.com)

Teacher Tube is media sharing that works like YouTube and is even designed to resemble it visually. However, as Teacher Tube is for educational purposes, the material and the comments contained therein are much less likely to contain inappropriate material. Some care is still required to ensure that content is appropriate for the specific age group as children of different ages use the site.

The classroom idea described above combines video and sound via which children can show their understanding of a process and herein lies the value of podcasting. The use of audio files that can be published to an authentic audience encourages children to carefully consider the use of dialogue in order to express themselves clearly so that they show their conceptual understanding. The activity also encourages children to consider their use and application of mathematical vocabulary.

McLeod and Vasinda (2009) express similar findings in their exploration of 'mathcasts', where students were asked to show their mathematical thinking via the use of Web 2.0 tools. They argue that these students were becoming consciously aware of problem solving strategies and making their thinking visible. The same authors found that a further benefit occurred when they placed the work online. This provided a stimulus for a conversation about the math problems that had been the subject of the mathscast. Placing the mathcast on a blog also allowed teachers to offer targeted feedback about a specific part of the maths problem, thereby helping to personalise the learning involved.

Podcasting can be used for a wide range of activities. Various applications might include a diverse array of opportunities. For instance, literacy orientated learning tasks like the production of stories are well suited to podcasting. In addition, the serial nature of podcasting lends itself to the creation of a school radio station where children can make daily or weekly broadcasts detailing events and people in the school community (Cole 2007). Podcasts are also a very good way to distribute learning materials to both pupils and teachers alike, as well as serving as another method of communicating with parents (Cole 2007). The next case study seeks to express some further learning outcomes that can be derived from podcasting.

Case study 1: story telling with podcasts (life in Victorian times 1)

Year 6 were studying Victorian Britain. Their particular focus for this topic centred on investigating the life of children from this time. The children were asked to research 'child labour' and the types of jobs children might have been required to undertake and they became especially interested in the jobs that children used to carry out in coal mines. The class was asked to find out about the life of a child who worked in a mine and the children undertook various activities to increase their knowledge and understanding of this subject. For example, they visited the website for the National Coalmining Museum (http://www.ncm.org.uk), where they were able to take a virtual tour to help them visualise mechanical equipment located at a coal mine. They studied some of the images of 'trappers' that were available and discovered other images that had been provided by the museum and put up on Flickr. The children also visited sites like the National Archives (http://www.nationalarchives.gov.uk) and the BBC primary history site: (http://www.bbc.co.uk/schools/primaryhistory/victorian_britain/s.gov.uk/education/default.htm).

Gradually, the pupils accumulated a collection of data and images relating to children working in coalmines. At this point the teacher extended the learning experience by playing the children an audio clip from the BBC School Radio service that recreated the life of a fictional child named 'Jimmy' (http://www.bbc.co.uk/schoolradio/subjects/history/victorians/trapper/first_day). This clip recounted the first day of the experience of a child labourer in a coal mine in the role of a trapper. After listening to the clip the teacher gave the children the task of continuing the story of the life of this child via the creation of a podcast. The children were required to work in pairs to create the next episode of the original story through the production of their own audio clips.

The resulting podcasts made by the children revealed certain features and demonstrated learning from different parts of the curriculum. In the execution of the podcast, the children had to make sure that they had used some of the historical content and knowledge that they had previously gathered during their research on the Victorians. Their podcast therefore demonstrated their understanding of the features of Victorian life. For instance, the children revealed their knowledge regarding the age of some of the children working in mines, the time of day the work was started and additional factual information on subjects like the food and drink consumed by miners.

Some podcasts showed that the children were aware of information about how the mine was made 'secure', through pit props, and demonstrated their understanding of other safety features employed to try and keep miners safe. They discussed how the coal might have been transported through the use of pit ponies and child labour and covered other issues including the methods used when miners traversed down the mine and what jobs children might have undertaken while being employed as 'putters' and 'trappers'.

The podcasts enabled the children to show their factual knowledge of Victorian coalmining as well as demonstrating their grasp of 'what life was like in the past'. This feature of illustrating empathy and showing the ability to stand in the shoes of others is a desirable outcome from a history lesson, but an aspect of learning that can be hard to achieve. Here the dialogic nature of podcasts, which allowed for the capture of speech and the dramatic recreation of events in a coal mine, enabled the children to work in ways that promoted this objective. The best podcasts made by the class revealed a combination of factual knowledge and expressive language that helped build interest and suspense into their recreations.

In their exploration of podcasts, McLeod and Vasinda (2009) noted a similar outcome when capturing dialogue. The authors investigated the use of podcasts in relation to an exercise called 'Reader's Theatre', where voice projection and dynamics as well as expressive reading was used to convey meaning to text in order to improve fluency and comprehension. By podcasting, the children were able to engage a wider audience through their classroom activity and the resulting sense of performance increased motivation and engagement with the exercise. The children also enjoyed the permanency of the voice recordings, which allowed them to listen and re-listen to their recordings in order to improve their performance. This was described as an 'enchantment' of listening (McLeod and Vasinda 2009: 242). Halsey (2007: 101) also concluded that podcasts helped children to 'hone' both their speaking and listening skills as well as developing their reading ability.

The creation of the coalmining podcasts also required the children to write a 'playscript' detailing the action before the episode could be recorded. This requirement reveals another hidden benefit of this tool. The children needed to spend a considerable time drafting out their thoughts in order to create a viable story and were required to consider the structure, sequence and dramatic pace of their writing. In addition, the children needed to consider the application of issues like 'who might talk when' and how their thoughts could be best conveyed through the application of powerful expressive language. Podcasts, therefore, do not only require children to develop an expressive spoken vocabulary, but also to develop their writing skills. In addition, the fact that the podcasts are often published on a blog meant that the audience listening to the work were able to leave comments and this acted as a stimulus for reflection.

So far this podcasting exercise has shown how children might reveal their historical knowledge and their ability to use the spoken and written word, but it can also be seen to develop broader ICT capability. We came across the notion of capability in the chapter on Web 2.0 in the curriculum, where we defined it as the ability of children to use routines and skills in the use of ICT in order to achieve broader goals. In this exercise, children developed a number of skills relating to the creation of audio tracks, using free software like Audacity (http://audacity.sourceforge.net/) to record sound. They became familiar with routines involved in the process of editing their recordings and learnt how to convert sound files and export them in MP3 format, which meant that their work could be uploaded to the internet as podcasts. With just a little experimentation the children were able to combine sound clips, delete unwanted features, add sound effects and 'playback' their files to consider how they might improve them. In doing so they were not only learning skills, but learning how to participate in a creative form of communication that they could employ in a number of different contexts.

As well as commenting on the acquisition of knowledge and skills in relation to specific curriculum areas it is also worth noting the general levels of engagement exhibited by children using this technology. Proponents of podcasting in the primary classroom note the stimulation and motivation of the children involved. Cole (2007) cites headteacher Vanderpuye as stating that 'podcasting' had transformed her school. She felt that all schools should be undertaking the activity, for it would seem that the variety of skills involved in the creation of podcasts combine to offer deep level learning experience. These skills reflect the podcast's cross-curricular nature and its effect on participation levels and collaboration via team approaches, not to mention levels of personal satisfaction and achievement. Indeed, Halsey (2007: 101) found that her use of podcasts with children, to record their weekly learning experiences, allowed them to reflect on their learning and move from making comments about surface learning to deeper engagement in meta-cognition.

When introducing children to podcasting it might be advisable to encourage them to listen to some that have already been made by other young people. This will stress to the pupils the nature of 'podcasting etiquette'. They will then begin to appreciate the virtues of organising their thoughts so that they know when to speak, not interrupting or speaking over their peers and making sure that they speak clearly. Pupils might also consider features like suitable duration times and how to capture and maintain the interest of the audience. For example, they are likely to conclude that shorter podcasts are more engaging.

Case study 2: podcasting for assessment (life in Victorian times II)

In Chapter 4 we discussed the potential of Web 2.0 tools in relation to the personalisation of learning. We considered the possibility of using Web 2.0 in order to provide an increased array of assessment tools, although this sentiment, we argued, was still yet to be fully realised in the primary classroom. Austin and Anderson (2008: 94) suggest that 'assessment is the Achilles heel of ICT embedding in e-schooling' and compound this statement by saying that 'assessment remains unfit for purpose not only for today's ICT enhanced-classroom, but also for tomorrow's transformed one' (ibid.). As podcasting becomes more widespread in the primary classroom, it might be that, as well as providing an engaging way to capture dialogue, it could also be used as a helpful assessment tool. The following case study illustrates how this might work.

The previous case study focused on a Year 6 class studying Victorian childhood. It detailed how podcasting could help children show their knowledge and understanding of a period in history as well as revealing the ability of the pupils to consider the emotions and experiences of people who lived in the past. In this case study we concentrate on some of the 'skills' that are uniquely associated with the curriculum subject of history. The children involved in this case study were asked to study a photograph of a group of people from the Victorian period. The picture portrayed a Victorian family. The male adult in the family was a cricketer and his cricket bat was given a prominent place in the photograph. His wife and his seven children were the other main features of the picture and although they would have been considered privileged and moderately wealthy, they are fairly representative of families who were photographed in the period.

The children were initially shown the photograph on an interactive whiteboard and asked to study it, but no other information was given at this stage. They were then asked to work in pairs and to a make a list of questions that they could ask of the source. Next, the children were required to make a podcast detailing their investigation and enquiry into the picture and recorded what they thought the picture was about and why it might have been taken. More importantly, they were asked to discuss how they could use the picture to investigate Victorian life and the teacher set them a quest to see if they could try to make 'deductions' about the past.

The children engaged in the task and discussed several different features of the photograph. These included issues like the differences between the ways that Victorian children dressed and the ways that young people dress today. They also discussed themes like the number of children in the family and concluded that families in Victorian times might have been bigger than they are today. They considered the issue that the people in the photograph did not look very happy as they were not smiling, although this was perplexing for the children in the class. It was concluded that the family looked wealthy because of the type of dress they were wearing and, at the end of their podcasts, some of the children posed additional questions for further investigation. They could not work out the significance of the cricket bat in the picture, for example, and they were unsure as to the gender of some of the very young children. They could not decide if they were 'dressed' as girls or boys.

In this case study the podcast provides a very important tool. It captures the thought processes of the children in a way that is difficult to achieve when children are asked to write. In the classroom an assessment might typically take the form of a written product. Children have to work hard at translating their thoughts and questions into writing, when they might be able to express them clearly and in detail through speech. They may find it rather laborious to record all their lines of enquiry, particularly if they are not motivated by the written word and their written work may not reflect the full extent of their understanding as a result. Younger children in particular are unlikely to sustain the level of concentration required for the completion of substantial written assignments and this is compounded when they lack the written vocabulary to express themselves. The podcast provides a good tool to capture the thinking of the children and it provides a type of assessment that is more likely to reveal the developing historical skills of pupils directly.

This last point is important as it can be argued that, in many cases, assessment serves to capture a picture of the knowledge that children have accumulated in a curriculum subject, but fails to focus on the important themes of skills and conceptual understanding. It might be suggested that assessments that emphasise skills development are more useful to the educator than those that only reveal the knowledge base of the children. Much knowledge learnt at a young age may be forgotten or become redundant, whereas the application of a skill maybe honed and developed for future years. However, in order to demonstrate a skill one needs to use it and where a child finds it harder to engage with a written activity they are more likely to perform below their potential. In the case of skills relating to historical enquiry at least, it is likely that podcasting offers children a way of expressing themselves that makes it easier to articulate the underlying processes and concepts.

This case study is just one example of how a Web 2.0 tool might be employed to offer new scope to the formulation and administration of assessment. This supports the argument previously presented by Green *et al.* (2005: 26) in their comments on personalisation and their advocacy of different types of assessment for younger children that move away from 'exam based assessment of a prescribed body of knowledge'.

The photograph described in this case study can be accessed at: http://www.nationalarchives.gov.uk/education/lessons/730-popup.htm.

Practical task 1

- If you have never previously engaged with a podcast, try listening to some online. There are thousands available covering a range of interests. Try subscribing to some favourite sites so that podcasts will be automatically downloaded by locating the relevant RSS feed.
- Try and locate some educational podcasts. For instance, the Education Podcast Network (http://epnweb.org/) is a good starting point. This site provides a gateway to a range of educational subject-specific podcasts.
- Go to the Audacity website and download the software to your PC (http://audacity.sourceforge.net/).
- Try making a recording yourself and then see how easy it is to edit your voice files.
- Consider all the potential uses of podcasting for the pupils in your classroom.

Reflective task 1

Consider the potential for the use of podcasting to achieve positive results in terms of digital literacy. In the second case study in this chapter it was suggested that children should be shown examples of young people's podcasts in order to clarify good practice. Children should be able to evaluate the medium themselves, identifying positive attributes and areas in which improvements are possible. This would help to encourage the development of critical and reflective faculties, particularly in reference to digital and online media. Consider how you would manage this part of the lesson.

Case study 3: science investigations on Myebook (presenting digital projects 1)

Tool focus

Myebook (http://www.myebook.com)

Myebook is a free tool that enables users to combine a variety of media into a book style presentation that combines a page by page display with a satisfying page turning effect. This allows children to publish an authentic looking e-book to a high production standard, incorporating their own work, resources provided by the teacher and web content. Minimal information is required in order to sign up and despite a slightly commercial style of interface design the site is easy to use. Once you have signed up you can go to the

Myebooks section to create a new e-book, specify a number of pages, choose a decorative theme and then get started. Material including images, video, sound, files and flash content are added by uploading them to 'galleries' and then dragging the resources from the relevant gallery to any position on a blank page or a designated region of a template, called a 'theme'. There are other tools to explore as well, and additional features in menus that are conventionally located along the top bar. When using these tools look out for the properties tool panel on the right hand side of the screen. This allows you to configure many features, such as adding hyperlinks to hotspots or customising the colours and properties of shapes.

Year 4 were studying healthy eating for their science topic for the term. This topic lasted for six weeks, during which time the class investigated food groups and categories of food such as healthy, neutral and undesirable foods. They studied nutritional terminology such as protein, fats, carbohydrates, vitamins and minerals. They discovered the results of eating too much of any one food group and of eating processed food. The project culminated in the class preparing a healthy 'school meal'. It also allows more than one dish to be prepared as a representative sample of foods enjoyed within the class.

The teacher had planned the topic in a way that ensured the children would create a wide variety of different resources. He wanted a way of bringing all these resources into one place and wanted a means of sharing the results of the children's work with other schools doing similar projects. For this purpose he selected the Myebook tool.

During the term the pupils produced the following resources to demonstrate their understanding of the topic. They produced posters showing healthy food groups. They wrote meal plans for the three main meals of the day. They kept a food diary and recorded what food groups they most commonly ate. They explored where different foods might come from by looking at the labels on food packets and they recorded the origins and journeys undertaken by the products on world maps. They further studied food labels to find out about the content of processed food, particularly observing information like sugar and salt content. They found out about preservatives and additives and how these were denoted on packaging. They discussed calorie intake, noting the different calorie requirements of each gender and they learnt new terms like saturated and unsaturated fats. This information was recorded in annotated fact files.

This was followed up by some experiments, including one that demonstrated the detrimental effect of sugar on tooth enamel and one where children undertook blindfolded food tasting to see if they could identify different flavours and food groups. The children recorded the results of these experiments and created glossaries based on the new vocabulary they had learnt during the term. In some cases these were recorded in writing and in other instances by using digital sound recorders. The children also undertook observational drawings of fruits, using chalk pastels and, in response to being shown the work of Arcimboldo, they created portraits and pictures on various themes using different fruit and vegetables.

As the children created the resources resulting from the activities described above, they uploaded their work into the galleries on Myebook. Pictures, sound recordings and written work were therefore lodged on the site ready to be reviewed and used at the appropriate time. As the time approached when the children were due to plan and prepare their healthy 'school meal' the teacher knew that it would be important to reprise all the stages of the topic covered so far. Children would draw on all of these experiences in this final task. The children were therefore asked to create an e-book, drawing on the resources that they had uploaded. The teacher had already inserted templates on to some pages and had labelled them so as to lend some structure and to ensure that the children covered all the necessary aspects of the topic. However considerable scope remained for the children to determine the final organisation and presentation of the information.

Having completed this stage the children undertook to plan the meal that they were going to cook and, with the help of the teacher, prepared to video it. The children were told that they should nominate two people to prepare the food and that faces should not appear in the video. With the teacher on hand to supervise, the children videoed all the stages of presentation, such as measuring ingredients and this was edited into a short video that was inserted as the final page in the e-book.

Classroom idea 2: international exchange (presenting digital projects II)

If other schools, from other countries perhaps, had agreed to pursue this project in a coordinated way, children would have then been able to share their project more widely and would have been able to see how the same considerations around nutrition and well-being led to very different food choices in different cultures.

Digital e-books have similar benefits to learning situations as other Web 2.0 tools addressed. In this case study children are learning to work collaboratively, problem solving and combining a variety of media that will encourage them to use their higher order learning skills as well as demonstrating their capabilities. However, what makes this project innovative is the potential to share work with children from different cultures. This 'connectedness' helps to encourage respect for and understanding of diverse communities. It also gives the children a window on the wider world where learning can be seen as a pan-cultural activity not something that only occurs within the confines of the classroom. In addition, as the children are obliged to anticipate an international audience for their work, they are encouraged to consider the cultural diversity in their own class. This project therefore helps to address issues of personal identity, belonging, society and citizenship.

Classroom idea 3: social bookmarking in the classroom

Tool focus

Delicious (http://www.delicious.com)

Delicious is a popular social bookmarking site. One must sign up in order to use it, but this is free and very little personal information is required. Once you have access you can either install a toolbar in your browser or – if you do not want to do this, or if you are accessing the account from a computer other than your own – you can build a list of bookmarks using tools on the web page itself. This involves copying and pasting the web address of the site that you want to import and adding key items of 'meta-data'. This meta data consists of keywords that classify the website, known as 'tags' and a short amount of text that describes the site, which is typically used by users in order to explain why they have chosen to add it.

In these case studies we have used a number of websites and web based resources. Increasingly, classroom activities involve this sort of material and children will be exposed to a wide variety of web pages. This presents an opportunity to address issues of digital literacy and, specifically, to develop critical skills in the use of the web as an information space.

Social bookmarking sites can be used to create a repository of web resources and children can be encouraged to add to this collection whenever they use a new site. The use of the social bookmarking sites would therefore be integrated into a wide variety of tasks. The class teacher would create an account on a popular bookmarking site like Delicious, which would then be used by the whole class. Each time a site is added the children would be required to label it using 'tags' and therefore consider how the site is classified, with reference to content, style and purpose. They would also annotate the entry, indicating the attributes of the site that bear on relevance and quality.

The skills employed in this exercise are identical to those that children need to develop in order to become discriminating users of the World Wide Web. They will also help children develop as effective users of blogs, wikis and other Web 2.0 tools that also need to be classified and will be scrutinised in a similarly analytical way. It therefore bears directly on the quality of their own work. This repository can also be used subsequently as a collection of web resources that children can search and explore safely in the course of independent enquiry.

Chapter 6

Children as explorers

This chapter covers the following:

- connecting Web 2.0 with the subject areas of citizenship and globalisation;
- how children might use Web 2.0 as a window on the world;
- exploring further the connection between Web 2.0 and the constructivist education paradigm.

In the third chapter of the last section we encountered a number of theories that emphasised the importance of giving children autonomy in relation to the learning process. It was suggested that one of the ways in which this could be expressed was to try and move from a form of teaching that 'fed' information to children to one in which children 'fished' for it in more active and independent ways. Within this context we encounter the principle that learning to ask appropriate questions and to develop methods and strategies of enquiry was of equal importance to 'learning' knowledge in a mechanistic sense.

We now turn to the notion of children as 'explorers'. In particular, we use this chapter to consider the role of Web 2.0 tools in order to help children to engage with the wider world. The child's world should no longer be limited by the physical confines of the classroom walls. Children should now be using technology to look beyond their immediate vicinity in order to learn from a more diverse array of experiences. Technology should be used to help learners access virtual territory so that they interact with the community outside school, become aware of national and international issues and engage with the broader themes of globalisation. Indeed, the role of the internet in encouraging this type of learning cannot be underestimated. Here, the links with the global aspects of the citizenship agenda need to be acknowledged and the teacher needs to be able to realise the opportunity Web 2.0 gives for children to achieve some of the themes associated with this subject.

Interestingly, features typically related to citizenship education share commonalities with Web 2.0 technologies. For instance, Claire and Woolley (2007) define the characteristics of citizenship education. Amongst others, the concepts and skills named include critical thinking, participation, enquiry and investigation, empowerment and having a voice that is heard. These are all areas of learning we have discussed in relation to the new technologies that feature in this text. These authors go on to note that effective, creative citizenship teaching is composed of:

mirrors and windows and roots and wings. Mirrors are needed to reflect our world, and windows opening out to wider horizons and possibilities; roots so that we know who we are and feel strongly connected, and wings so that we can fly, fantasise, hope and dream.

(Claire and Woolley 2007: 154)

The very heart of Web 2.0 is defined by users adding information about their worlds and encouraging the notion of connectedness. This type of technology can provide the 'mirror' so that children are not unaware or misinformed. In a sense it can also provide the 'wings' by which children can access distant horizons, it enables them to participate and to contribute a voice that is heard.

Austin and Anderson (2008: 97) continue with this discussion by stating that one of the most innovative areas of e-schooling is how it can make citizenship education real for young people. Here, they acknowledge the potential of ICTs, which consist of formally recognised educational tools as well as social software applications that are employed more widely on the web. They discuss this in relation to schools within Ireland when they examine how cross-community tensions had ruptured the flow of daily contact between young people and created persistent difficulties in providing an education in citizenship. They track the use of ICT to create partnerships between schools, which were instrumental in breaking down barriers between children.

In addition, this technology also helped to eradicate barriers of a different kind. Schools in Ireland saw digital technology being used to form connections between SEN schools and children in mainstream settings. Austin and Anderson (2008) further connect their findings to the broader international perspective by discussing how the e-Twinning programme was used to promote social inclusion and build bridges. They conclude that there is certainly a case for ICT educational policy to be closely aligned with wider social and political goals.

Global citizenship and new technologies cannot be discussed without considering the link to the geography curriculum. It would appear that geographical teaching of the global dimension is underdeveloped in school. Indeed, OFSTED (2008: 45) note that:

Most primary school schemes of work give insufficient explicit consideration to the global dimension. Where it occurs, the emphasis tends to be on place rather than global interdependence or the connectivity of places themselves.

They note that 'acting locally, thinking globally' is a cornerstone of the global dimension and advocate that schools should explore strategies to achieve this aim. The authors discuss how only a few schools teach the global dimension adequately by exploiting the potential of partnership with schools abroad. They suggest that links between pupils, when acting as pen pals for example, can be very productive when well supported and sustained. It is here that Web 2.0 technologies offer new opportunities to teachers and help children to think globally. Tools like eTwinning and videoconferencing allow children to develop 'penpal' like relationships in a more immediate and sophisticated manner that is perhaps better suited to the pupils of the digital generation.

While this chapter studies children as 'explorers' in a geographical sense, it also defines the theme of 'exploration' from a pedagogical viewpoint. The first paragraph refers to children 'fishing' for meaning and exploring how information is pieced together in order to make meaning. We have seen that these terms derive from a constructivist view of learning and teaching, but it is not always easy to comprehend how the principles and theories associated with constructivism apply to practice within classroom activities. In order to help clarify this situation we intend to use a framework developed by DfES (2004), in which 17 distinct elements of a constructivist learning environment are described. In doing so we also follow Pritchard's analysis, which emphasises specific applications for ICT within that structure (Pritchard 2007: 86). Pritchard uses these characteristics to promote good pedagogical practice in relation to ICT and the internet. We propose to extend this framework with a specific pedagogical focus, so as to emphasise the role of Web 2.0 tools as a means of promoting exploration, enquiry, enablement and empowerment.

The characteristics of constructivism identified by the DfES (2004) are as follows:

- multiple perspectives;
- pupil-directed goals;
- teachers as coaches;
- meta-cognition;
- learner control;
- real-world activities and contexts;
- knowledge construction;
- sharing knowledge;
- reference to what pupils know already;
- problem solving;
- explicit thinking about errors and misconceptions;
- exploration;
- peer-group learning;
- alternative viewpoints offered;
- scaffolding;
- assessment for learning;
- primary sources of data.

For now we are going to leave this list but we will come back to it at the end of the chapter and identify where the aspects of constructivism can be observed in the case studies detailed below:

Case study 1: historical and geographical enquiry

Tool focus

History Pin (local history investigation)

History Pin is a Web 2.0 service that represents a merging of several different sources of information. At its heart is an expanding archive of photographs of different geographical locations, from various historical periods. However, the power of this tool is encountered in the way in which the archive is accessed. By combining with Google, History Pin allows users to locate photographs on a version of Google Maps that has thumbnails mounted or 'pinned' on it. By zooming into the map the user is able to identify photographs within increasingly precise locations. In this respect, the service is similar to Flickr, but the content is very suitable for use in the classroom. In the spirit of Web 2.0 users are also able to upload photographs, thereby extending the archive, and can even attach stories to them, creating an additional layer of information to the map. Another feature that has the potential to aid learning is the recently added street view facility which allows the user to access a 360 degree photographic representation of many areas, by dragging an icon to a location on the map.

This case study was designed for a Year 5 class and created opportunities for a cross-curricular topic based on local history. Children were finding out about how their community had changed over the last century using History Pin. This allowed them to find pictures of their neighbourhood and contrast these with modern-day views of the same area via 'street view'. Children were then asked to seek out other pictures that depicted the local area in the past. They were asked to talk to parents and to obtain copies of photographs that could be scanned and to find out about the stories behind the photographs. The children were then asked to compose short stories which accompanied the photographs when they were uploaded to the History Pin site.

Using the processes described above, the children were able to create a digital history book that could be accessed by the wider school community, children from partner schools, family members and – ultimately – the History Pin community. This last point raises an important issue as the teacher had to be careful to ensure that children did not disclose any personal information about themselves. She was open about this requirement and ensured that the children understood the main issues involved. They were asked not to bring photographs containing children who could be recognised or identified as a result and the teacher asked the children to read their written compositions to the class, which allowed her to verify that the content was suitable.

This activity has a number of important outcomes from a learning perspective. Children were encouraged to develop practical skills around historical and geographical enquiry using an online tool that is, in other contexts, used regularly in day to day life. At the same time, the History Pin environment provided rich stimulus for the exercise and scope for children to frame their own questions. This was achieved thanks to the central role played by the photographs that children selected from their own personal family history, which could be readily incorporated into a rich, interactive multimedia resource. The tool allowed the children to encounter history in the context of story-telling, a useful mechanism which helped them to remain engaged and provided a meaningful context for historical investigation. It also allowed the children involved to juxtapose their story with that of others.

What is more, in creating a digital resource that could be accessed on the web, History Pin provided an excellent vehicle for an investigation that could be developed through ongoing conversations with family members. The fact that this resource could potentially go on to acquire a life of its own in the hands of a wider audience created an exciting dimension to the project and established an authentic and meaningful extension to the children's work.

Case study 2: extending the use of journey sticks

Tool focus

Glogster (http://edu.glogster.com)

Glogster is a Web 2.0 tool that allows members to create posters using a suite of easy to use tools and a large selection of pleasing graphics. Users can upload their own materials in the form of images or video and can then incorporate these on to a virtual poster, which can then be saved and shared, selectively, with others in the community. One of the nicest features of the Glogster site is the floating toolbar, which provides some quite sophisticated customisation tools (e.g. shadow control) without compromising the accessibility of the basic features. It is therefore usable by children of various ages. By using Glogster you agree to allow other users to reuse and repurpose your work, so some care needs to be taken around the use of copyrighted work. Forum postings are also not screened, so some care may need to be taken in relation to the use of these tools.

This case study is derived from the geographical classroom exercise of journey sticks. More information about this can be found from a video on Teachers' TV if this is an unfamiliar activity (Teachers TV 2008). The principle of the journey stick is that children create a physical record of their journey, which can then be used as a visual prompt to help them sequence the route and as a stimulus for recalling how they felt on the journey, creating a link to emotional responses as well as spatial relationships. Children are asked to find a large stick to which they stick 'mementos' of a route they have taken. Typical exemplar objects might include leaves or other kinds of vegetation, seeds and nuts or even items of rubbish.

In this case study the children selected and created their journey sticks in the usual way, but upon returning to the classroom were asked to photograph the stick and then to disassemble it, taking care to keep all the objects in order. Each object was then photographed in preparation for creating the map. In this instance the teacher put children into mixed ability pairs and supplied each pair with an image file depicting an outline map of the area in which they had walked. This was to be uploaded on to a 'glog' as a starting point. The children then uploaded their photographs and positioned them around the map, using lines to indicate the precise locations in which they were discovered. Each glog therefore contained a map and photographs of the objects from two children's journey sticks.

Having done this, the children were asked to create lines from each picture, leading to a text-field that contained descriptions of their feelings about the journey and the objects they had discovered. The children were required to select a design of text-field that was different from that of their partner and to ensure that they used that design throughout. In this way the work of individual children could be identified easily from within their collaborative presentation. As a final step the children uploaded their pictures of the journey sticks as they had been photographed prior to being disassembled and added these to the overall presentation, along with a short piece of reflective writing about the journey they had made.

In this exercise the Web 2.0 tool was used to aid in the creation of a durable resource based on the experience of creating the journey stick, which gave scope for individual creative expression. The format also encourages children to realise and reflect upon the unique and personal nature of the journey they have made, a feature of the activity that is promoted by the organisation of children into pairs.

It also allowed children to work in an online environment that promoted sharing with schools from other regions and even other countries. This activity, which can be conducted almost anywhere, stimulates awareness of the local environment on a number of different levels: of the landscape and built environment, of the details of flora and other objects encountered while walking and of cultural and even economic characteristics. By allowing this exercise to be represented in such a visually stimulating way and by allowing the results to be shared so readily, Glogster promotes opportunities for children to access a powerfully informative perspective on the local conditions experienced in distant places. This aspect of the activity is enhanced by the incorporation of emotive and reflective writing.

The experience of journey sticks struck a chord with the children, who started to produce Glogs about the journeys they made when visiting places on holiday. These were then shared with the class, which added an informative extension to the original exercise. As the Glogs produced by the children increased in number, the class were able to create a map noting the locations in the world of all the journeys that had been made. This provided a useful resource by which children could extend their knowledge and understanding of the globe.

Classroom Idea 1: Wordle-scapes (exploring distant places 1)

Tool focus

Wordle (http://www.wordle.com)

Wordle is a very simple but pleasing application which takes blocks of texts and processes them as a jumble of the most regularly recurring words. The words are oriented vertically and horizontally and the size of each word depends upon the number of times it occurs in the text. To get started, go to the Wordle website and select the 'create' option. Then paste a block of text into the top textbox and click 'go'. Alternatively you can 'wordle' a website by entering the URL into the next text field and clicking the 'Go' button for that field. This provides a great way of analysing a piece of text in a way that allows the teacher to immediately focus in on key terms, and a stimulating way of initiating discussion.

The following idea was inspired by a teacher's TV programme on distant places (Teachers TV 2010). We have used this concept and extended it to include a Web 2.0 dimension. Children in a Year 4 class are exploring the geographical theme of distant places. As an introduction to the topic the children are shown a picture and asked to describe what they can see. To help them in this process the teacher asks the class to trace the outline of the scene, which helps the children to analyse a complex picture by identifying distinct regions that can be scrutinised in isolation from one another. Drawing on their observations of the original picture the children create a 'word-scape' by writing descriptive words about the things they observe or sensations or activities that can be inferred from the visual stimulus. For example, one area within the outline representation of the postcard might contain nouns like 'beach', 'shore', 'shells' and 'boats', but also 'fishing' and 'windy'.

The children are encouraged to use expressive vocabulary that denotes colour – terms like 'emerald' and 'turquoise' to describe the sea, for example – and to explore vocabulary that could describe the physical geography of the place in an expressive way. The teacher also emphasises the importance of exploring the character of human influence on the landscape and in this way the word-scape serves as the basis for a more systematic and wide-ranging analysis of the image than would occur if children were simply asked to talk about it. Importantly, children are told that they should repeat words in different areas of the word-scape and that it is important to try and describe everything in each region.

Having completed this stage of the process the children are asked to enter all the words that they had used into a wordle. If they had used a word more than once they were told to type that word the requisite number of times as well. In creating the wordle they were invited to play around with the colours, fonts and arrangements used, generating new wordles until they were happy with the overall effect. This can be done in a controlled way using a series of easy to use menus, but a fun alternative is provided by a simple-to-use 'randomise' button.

The resulting wordles represent an effective synthesis of the analysis that the children had conducted. The overall effect is colourful and variations in orientation and size provide children with an alternative way of engaging with text; one focused on expressive vocabulary and which privileges the most relevant words. Critically, when set alongside the original photograph, they demonstrate the potential of descriptive language to evoke place in a way that is more accessible to the child than an equivalent piece of prose would be. Some of the vocabulary used in the wordles is also likely to suggest a starting point for the direction of the geographical enquiry of the distant place being studied.

The wordles themselves can then be displayed, allowing pupils to use the wordles of other children as a means of quickly analysing the visual information in complicated

Figure 6.1 A wordle based on one of the paragraphs in this chapter

and exotic pictures that they had not seen before. This further reinforces the message about the power of descriptive language in a compelling way and allows the children to compare their work with that of others. Once the topic has been completed the children can repeat the exercise and, in doing so, express their knowledge of themes associated with the distant place. Finally, the children considered both of their wordles, which provided an excellent visual record of how much more vocabulary and knowledge they had acquired over a sequence of lessons.

Classroom idea 2: variation on word-scapes (exploring distant landscapes II)

Tool focus

Twitter (http://twitter.com/); Twitpic (http://twitpic.com/) and TweetDeck (http://www.tweetdeck.com/)

Twitter is a micro-blogging service that allows people to form networks around personal or shared message streams. Each message is limited to 140 characters and can only contain basic text, which imposes a structure on communication and makes it accessible and easy to fit around other activities. A person monitors their own 'tweets' and those of other people on their network from a personal homepage on the Twitter website. Twitpic is a sister site that allows users to upload pictures with short text labels. Once you have joined Twitpic you can upload pictures via e-mail, using an account that is generated for you automatically and provided at registration.

Twitter does need to be used with care. Much of the content on the wider network is inappropriate for children and the website's own terms and conditions limit membership to individuals over the age of 13. Children should not be encouraged to create their own accounts, therefore, and steps must be taken to restrict access when using the service in class. Fortunately there are free to use applications that can help to manage safe and easy use. One example of this is an 'app' called Tweetdeck, which effectively filters the network so that only tweets from a specified account or which contain specified keywords are displayed.

This last feature is very powerful. Keywords can be constructed in such a way as to ensure uniqueness and defined as a 'hashtag' by putting a hash symbol at the front, e.g. #web2Exercise. The teacher can then create a column on the tweetdeck desktop that only displays messages containing this tag. This allows networks to form in this dynamic environment and to be able to communicate easily and safely. However, it is important to check that a tag is unique, by using it in a Twitter search first and to make hashtags very specific, using numbers or other symbols, perhaps, to avoid accidental contamination from other users.

In this variant of the previous activity, children from different schools take photographs of their local environment. They must first discuss this aspect of the task, deciding what the photograph needs to contain in order to be representative of the local environment and culture. These photographs are then exchanged with other schools, either via Twitpics or by another networking service such as the e-twinning site.

In order to manage the Twitpics option the teachers should use a tweet application, such as tweetdeck, so as to limit the children's view of the wider network, and should ensure that they are on hand to directly supervise these aspects of the task. By projecting the connection to the Twitter site on to the whiteboard when it is being used, it becomes easier to monitor this. Teachers could agree a hashtag for the exercise, e.g. #wordleScapes2011 and create a column on the Tweetdeck desktop that only displays search results containing this unique term. This means that all the photographs can be easily accessed along with other messages relating to the task. For example, once a school has selected a photo they would tweet, using the same hashtag, thanking the authors and effectively claiming that image for their part in the activity.

In cases where schools are already connected via an online network they can use that service just as easily. The e-twinning website, for example, has a desktop tool that allows members to share resources and to communicate via a blog. In either case, this method is more effective than e-mail as the communication and exchange between schools is consolidated into a single resource, rather than being distributed across several uncoordinated e-mails.

Having obtained a photograph from a school – preferably one located in a region that has a very different natural and cultural environment – the wordscape exercise is conducted along the lines described above. The wordles that are created as a result are then converted into images and returned to the school that created them. The easiest way to do this is to press the print screen button while the Wordle is being viewed and paste the screenshot into MS paint. The image can then be cropped and saved as an image file so that it can be posted back to Twitpics in order to be collected. Put very simply, each school submits a photograph of their local area and receives a wordle in return.

The purpose of this variation is to create a reflective dimension according to which children think critically about their own local environment and ultimately see how people from distant places describe it. This can enhance the original activity, by providing an insight into the importance of cultural perspectives on perceptions of the world and can stimulate children to look at their own local area in a different way. The wordles from other schools can also provide the starting point for discussion about the possibilities and limitations of descriptive language.

Case study 3: Marvel superhero squad (sequencing speech I)

Tool focus

Marvel superhero squad show (http://superherosquad.marvel.com)

The Super Hero Squad website supports the creation of short comic strips and full length books. The user selects different arrangements of frames for their presentation and then inserts backgrounds, characters and props into them. Dialogue can be added in a range of different callouts, or can be simply superimposed on the picture, while sound effects can be added in the form of visual text representations. This promotes awareness of the importance of sequence as an element in storytelling and as a narrative device. What is more, since text can be inserted in the form of commentary, speech and thought and is always juxtaposed with visual depictions of scene and action, this tool creates opportunities to explore questions of inference and interpretation. Children must consider how to communicate a message to the reader with a limited set of tools and a strictly limited amount of space. In addition to this, setting the story within the context of a Marvel comic strip requires engagement with the principle of genre and the visual approach to literacy and storytelling might appeal to and engage reluctant writers. Nevertheless, it also provides the more able with a new and stimulating context for creative expression.

Web 2.0 has created some very interesting and appealing applications that are free for everyone to use. There is a huge range of tools, of varying quality, but some do support an array of learning opportunities by providing occasions for creative expression. The following case study illustrates how one such application achieves this through a multimedia approach that would have been hard to obtain with traditional ICTs, even a few years ago. It uses the Super Hero Squad Show website, which allows children to create comic strips of varying length and therefore supports the use of visual presentation in story telling. It also gives prominence to dialogue and therefore allows children to explore the potential of speech as a way of developing narrative.

The class starts the lesson by reading and talking about a variety of comics. The teacher asks the children to pull out some common themes that characterise the genre: the importance of visual images, for example; the use of short, sharp sentences and the representation of sound effects. Attention should be drawn to the prominence of action and characters and to specific devices, such as the distinction between speech bubbles and thought bubbles. Of central importance is sequence and this exercise is intended to exemplify how story telling relies on the construction and interlinking of sequences of scenes. Children are introduced to a superhero or heroine who never sleeps, but protects the school without anyone knowing. It is left up to the class to decide what he or she is called and exactly what superpowers they should have and a short period of time is allocated to this phase of the task.

Once this is done the teacher divides the class into pairs and each is allocated a number of hours within a 24 hour period. Each group then goes on to the Marvel Super Hero Squad Site, selects 'comic strip' and devises a scene depicting the work of their superhero(ine) at the time they are given. Even though the superhero(ine) does not sleep, the children must consider the time of day and the kinds of things that are happening at that time, basing the events on the kinds of activities that take place during the school day.

Meanwhile a wikipage is created, providing a space where the comic strips can be arranged into a continuous sequence. Once the strips are completed, the teacher can download them from the site, but should be aware that they will be saved as a PDF file. In order to make it easier to consolidate the scenes on the wiki, it is recommended that the teacher creates screenshots, using the print screen button on the keyboard and crops them in an application like MS paint. This means that they can be saved as discrete image files that can be easily uploaded to the wiki and combined.

While the teacher is doing this, the children should print off their strip and, as a whole class, read their story. They will realise that they have a series of unconnected scenes, but some sort of narrative should emerge, following the rhythm of the school day. Children rotate printouts so that each pair is given the scene from the period following their own. They are then asked to go back to the computer and create a single box scene which links their own part of the story with the one that follows. In this box they are asked to write from the perspective of a narrator who is able to see and describe everything, including the feelings and motives of the characters. In this way, a connected story is created from a set of unconnected scenes.

It could be observed that this sort of thing can already be achieved with other software applications like Kar2ouche, which allow children opportunities for storyboarding and visual literacy. In fact, this software provides a much more diverse range of content and more powerful 'animation' tools. However, the Web 2.0 context offers some additional advantages. For one thing it is free and highly accessible, and not just from school, but from outside as well. This means that work can develop overtime and in the context of homework and can be more readily shared. This is important as the child is aware of the implicit presence of a wider audience, which make the process of story telling more authentic, purposeful and engaging.

Additional classroom ideas: image hosting websites

We turn now to consider an array of image hosting websites. These types of sites more commonly go by the name of 'photosharing' sites, which allow users to publish their own digital photos in order to share them with a wider audience. Arguably the most famous example of this is Flickr, which we have encountered in previous discussions, but there are many others besides. Very many of the images on these sites have been added by public users and form the basis of a vast collection of visual material that can be utilised by a teacher. The potential advantage of these images is the diversity of the material available, which provides a useful alternative to educational image packs that are commonplace in school. The disadvantage of image hosting sites is the possibility of children meeting unsuitable content.

For this theme, instead of listing detailed case studies, we have presented a bulleted list of ideas for image sharing that can be extended and adapted to the individual's classroom.
Images could be used in the following ways:

- As a rich stimulus for story writing.
- Sites like Flickr are a very accessible source of pictures of geological features like, for instance, volcanoes.
- Flickr's world map facility can be used to see images from different countries around the world. For example, the class study of a distant place can be enhanced by accessing the world map and studying the photos that have been shared and uploaded by users in various locations in that country.
- Flickr's world map could also be used to help children find objects of physical and man-made significance (e.g. the Egyptian pyramids) in the world. Clues could be given by the teacher directing the children to that object. They could go on a 'treasure hunt' in order to find significant features pertaining to the country being investigated.
- Children could make a photoblog that shows images obtained on photosharing sites that show their developing view of a country under investigation.
- Sites like the Guardian Eyewitness http://www.guardian.co.uk/world/series/eyewitness can be used to promote curiosity and an understanding of the themes associated with citizenship. This site provides one image per day to users which portrays a visual representation of the major news event of the day. This could be very useful in

helping children to become aware of events that happen around the globe and to encourage them to form opinions of topical issues. At the start of the day a teacher could place the image on the interactive whiteboard and ask children to consider the meaning and importance of it.

- Sites like fotopedia http://www.fotopedia.com/ contain some very good high quality images that are organised into albums and so create collections of images on specific themes that can be shared with children. For instance, when searching on terms like 'Sikh' the user can access some fascinating pictures that could be used as the start of an enquiry into this religion.

Use of Microsoft Photostory 3
http://www.microsoft.com/windowsxp/using/digitalphotography/photostory/default.mspx

Moving on from image hosting websites, it is worthwhile spending a little time exploring an associated application that can manipulate digital photographs and help present them in a fascinating way.

Microsoft Photostory 3 is a free, internet sourced tool that can be downloaded on to a PC. Photostory lets a user sequentially display their digital photographs in a virtual storybook and add effects to them. The appeal of the software derives from the fact that it is extremely easy to use. To create a 'photostory', the user is guided through a series of simple steps. First, you are asked to import some of your digital images that you have previously collected on your PC. Once this has been achieved the selected pictures are displayed on a 'filmstrip' at the bottom of the screen. The order of the images, and therefore the sequence of a photostory, can be easily rearranged by clicking and dragging a picture to the desired place on the filmstrip. Each image can then be individually selected and enhanced in several ways. The pictures can be rotated and edited in terms of colour and tone. Text can be added to the images as well as audio files that give extra narrative or information. Next, you can opt for background music to give further dramatic quality. Finally, the user is given a number of options as to how the file might be saved and shared with a wider audience. Simple but complete photostories can be produced from scratch in a relatively short space of time.

Reflective task

- Consider the educational benefits of Photostory 3 in terms of encouraging good story structure and the use of narrative.
- Why is it of benefit for children to be able to record their own narration of their stories?
- What kind of ICT is being developed here?
- Consider how you might use this piece of software with your class.
- Why would this tool appeal to children?
- Are there any disadvantages when using Photostory 3?
- From what age do you think children could successfully use this tool?

Practical activity

- Download Photostory 3 and make a story of your own.

Before concluding this chapter we will now return to the theme of constructivism. We will review several of the processes and skills involved in some of the above case studies and match them to the characteristics of constructivist learning environments.

Table 6.1 Adapted from Pritchard (2007): the constructivist characteristics of Web 2.0 tools

Characteristics of Constructivism	Exemplars of constructivism
Multiple perspectives	History Pin: children were asked to find pictures of their neighbourhood and contrast these with modern day views of the same area via Google Map 'street view'.
Pupil-directed goals	In all the case studies children decide how to approach their work and the direction it might take.
Teachers as coaches	All the case studies detail activities where tasks are open-ended and children work with a good deal of autonomy.
Metacognition	Journey Sticks: children used glogs to reflect on their emotional responses to a journey and compare their feelings to others who made a similar trip.
Learner control	Children and teachers jointly responsible for many of the tasks defined in the case studies.
Real world activities and contexts	Image hosting websites like Guardian Eyewitness: children use daily images of news events to become aware of topical issues. History Pin: children used images sourced from their own communities and families.
Knowledge Construction	History Pin: children used photographs of the past and present to investigate change in the community.
Sharing knowledge	Journey sticks: children share glogs on their discovery of distance places.
Reference to what pupils already know	Sequencing speech: children start their online investigation of the comic-strip genre by perusing different comic books.
Problem solving	Classroom ideas for image hosting websites: children use Flickr's world map to conduct a treasure hunt to find significant natural and man-made landmarks around the world.
Explicit thinking about errors and misconceptions	Variations on Wordscapes: children send a picture of their community to partner schools who make a wordle based on this picture. They return the wordle to the children who can then assess different perceptions of place with their own characterisation of it.
Exploration	Wordle: exploration of a distant place via the creation of a wordscape and then a wordle.
Peer-group learning	Journey Sticks: children collaborate to produce a glog.
Alternative viewpoints offered	Variations on Wordscapes: children from different schools give an alternative perspective on the characteristics of a community.
Scaffolding	History Pin: children talk to parents and members of the local community to find out about pictures from the past. Wordle case study: structured, sequential learning where children make wordscapes of distant places before making a wordle.
Assessment for learning	Sequencing speech: children place their comic strips on a wiki and this would provide an ideal opportunity for others to peer assess work and offer suggestions for further improvements.
Primary sources of data	History Pin: children use pictures of the past as a basis for investigation.

Conclusion

This chapter contains some diverse case studies and classroom ideas and seeks to illustrate some of the best aspects of Web 2.0. Web 2.0 takes many guises and has so many different tools it may initially feel hard to know where to start in knowing which one to use. In addition, some Web 2.0 applications can have a limited life span and 'disappear' from the internet just as you are starting to enjoy using them. The tools discussed here have, however, been selected in order to show how they can make for open-ended, investigative and ultimately effective learning scenarios that accentuate a constructivist environment.

Chapter 7

Children as communicators

This chapter provides classroom ideas and case studies that illustrate how children can become effective communicators through the use of Web 2.0 tools. It covers:

- a description of the possible applications for blogs in a classroom setting;
- an assessment of blogs and wikis in relation to raising attainment in literacy;
- case studies using blogs, wikis and related communication tools.

In his work on distance-learning Moore (1991) discusses the term transactional distance as a 'space of potential misunderstanding' caused by differences – between student and teacher – in terms of values, personality, prior knowledge and cultural perspectives. While it could be said to apply to all courses, therefore, transactional distance is portrayed as something that concerns distance learning more directly than other types of education. The physical separation between the learner and teacher is presumed to magnify the impact of transactional distance to the point where specific strategies are required to overcome it. These strategies are traditionally conceived under the headings of *dialogue* – meaning opportunities for communication – and the teaching strategies, resources and learning environments created by the programme provider, which are referred to collectively as *structure*.

A tremendous amount of thought and effort has been invested in exploring the potential for technologies to overcome transactional distance and a large number, including a range of Web 2.0 tools, have been used to promote communication and to deliver materials within a well-structured environment. However, questions about the quality of dialogue and structure can be applied to any course and we might extend this observation and say any level of education as well, including primary school learning. In fact one could argue that transactional distance is a serious issue in the schooling of younger children given the very great gulf that exists between them and the teacher in terms of age, experience, cultural outlook and knowledge.

What is more, Moore himself observes that a simplistic analysis of the transactional distance, one that concerns itself solely with the structures and patterns of communication in a course, risks assuming that the learner is a fixed quantity and therefore misses the very real problems created by the very different needs, perspectives and prior experiences of individuals on the course (ibid.: 5). This is evidently a significant cause of transactional distance within primary schools as well.

Assuming that we acknowledge the existence of 'distance' as an obstacle to the kinds of 'transactions' involved in learning and teaching, it is necessary to consider the relevance of strategies relating to discourse and structure to primary teaching as well. In fact, it would probably not strike the reader as strange if we were to conclude that the success of learning in the primary classroom depended upon discovering and exploring as many opportunities as possible for communication. We have seen that other theorists have arrived at the same conclusion by other routes, the pedagogy of dialogic teaching for example (Bakhtin 1981 and Alexander 2004).

The notion of structure is a little harder to unpack within the context of the primary classroom, although few would oppose generalised comments about the importance of the learning environment. However, it is important to keep in mind the fact that the structure of a course refers to a notion of environment that exceeds, like the notion of distance, the purely physical. In this context structure refers to teaching strategies as well and all the apparatus within which communication takes place and how it is mediated: how dialogue is captured, for example, how roles are assigned, how rules are applied to conduct in and around conversation and how the purpose and objectives of communication are defined and agreed. In addition to this of course, it refers to the tools and the media that are provided to support communication, whether that be via the spoken or written word or by other forms of creative expression.

Following this line of thinking, it is natural to look at the role of the learning technologies again. As we saw earlier their role was initially conceived – in the context of distance learning at least – as a way of compensating learners for something they were missing. Technology-supported and internet based forms of communication were consequentially assumed to provide an impoverished means of communication relative to those encountered in face to face learning. However face to face learning does not necessarily provide learners with opportunities for rich dialogue, or a learning environment that is appropriately structured for their needs. This becomes particularly clear when one considers learners as varied individuals rather than a homogenous group.

In the third chapter of the previous section, we saw that the primary classroom can create obstacles for some individuals, for participation in learning generally and communication in particular. We explored some ways in which Web 2.0 tools could help to overcome these obstacles. The concept of transactional difference returns us to this point, for the role of learning technologies is not to provide surrogates for face to face, spoken communication or traditional forms of writing. Rather, Web 2.0 tools create new opportunities for communication in a realm that allows for more inclusive forms of dialogue, incorporating a wider, more diverse learning community and ready access to information from numerous sources. In many cases they can be seen to be the most elegant solution to issues around transactional distance since they provide means of communication and the structures needed to promote participation and to make that communication meaningful and constructive.

In this chapter we seek to explore the import of this last statement in more detail. We explore applications for Web 2.0 tools that help children emerge as communicators in their learning and how such tools help to create a constructive environment that maximises the impact of communication on learning.

Using blogs and wikis in the primary classroom

Blogs and wikis have already been the subject of considerable discussion in Section 1 of this book. However, of all the Web 2.0 tools available to the teacher and children, it would appear that blogs and wikis are the entities that are the most widely used in educational circles. As such, the different applications of blogs and wikis available to the primary practitioner are worthy of further consideration.

It is actually difficult to discuss 'blogs or wikis' as discrete phonomena with easily definable attributes. Take blogging for example. Blogs originally emerged as an online diary or personal journal where one person would update their blog with regular entries detailing particular notable events. However, as their appeal and popularity have grown, so have their uses. Blogs have many diverse purposes. Lankshear and Knoble (2008: 6) give an extensive, but not exhaustive, list of the type of weblogs that can be found. These include, to name but a few, personal diaries, journals, blogs that give a popularist view of events in the news, blogs that are used to sell products or to distribute news of that product, blogs that focus on hobbies and pastimes, blogs that are dedicated to detailing the activities of popular authors or band dates so that a fan base can keep track of new material. In addition to this there are cooking blogs, professional development blogs, photoblogs and audio blogs and many more. Indeed, so vast is the array of blogs that Davies and Merchant (2009) note that semantic content cannot be the determining factor that characterises a blog, but that their actual commonality can be found only in their similar textual layouts. The blog is defined by its form not its content, in other words.

Following the same trend, blogs have many different uses for the primary educationalist. Many schools now have a blog dedicated and maintained by each primary classroom in the school. Blogs such as these usually detail what the class have been studying during the school year and act as a kind of interactive newsletter for the community of the class. A teacher will usually upload examples of the work completed by the class to this blog. In addition, the practitioner might include audio clips of children singing or speaking a modern foreign language or even include video clips of the pupils performing activities like role plays. Of course, e-safety issues need to be considered here, but, handled carefully, this kind of activity becomes an opportunity to develop awareness of the risks among children and to reinforce understanding about safe and appropriate uses of internet and media technologies.

In this guise the blog acts as a very useful link between home and school, enabling parents to keep abreast of events occurring in class and to follow the achievements of their children. This is extremely valuable as, before the mechanisms of communication created by blogs and related technologies emerged, opportunities to look at work produced by the children were limited to open days, parents' evenings and homework books. The blog, therefore, provides ready and flexible access to the work of the school, helping to further establish and develop community links.

These types of blogs can have a further, less obvious, purpose. A classroom blog can provide the hook for a parent to talk to their child about school life and to maintain an ongoing dialogue about the progress of projects undertaken by the class. It is often very difficult for a parent to know exactly the nature of learning tasks that are being undertaken if their child is reluctant to discuss what is happening in school. It is not unusual for this to occur as many children prefer to keep their home and school lives as separate as possible. When asked about a school day a child may give a brief answer that acts as a 'filler' to sufficiently satisfy the parent but avoid other, additional conversation. Parents, can therefore use the blog to check what homework the child might have or to remind themselves of forthcoming trips, or just to keep abreast of the activities of the class.

For a working parent, a blog can be especially valuable. Often parents like these miss out on features of school life like family assemblies and parent–child teaching sessions, where the parent is invited into school to work alongside their child. The blog can act as a partner in learning, in this type of event, as it will provide a means by which the parent might at least be offered the opportunity to observe some of the results of the learning that took place at this time.

Blogs and wikis have been most widely used in the classroom as a way to inspire children to write in order to improve literacy standards. As with any new approach it is easy to be overzealous in expressing the benefits of this and care has been taken to portray a balanced view when discussing blogs and wikis in relation to raising attainment in literacy skills. There are, however, certain features of blogs and wikis that can be very useful to the primary practitioner and their quest to improve both reading and writing.

The World Wide Web provides children with a different form of communication from that offered by an exercise book. When electronic texts became available to read in school, children were attracted to the structure and presentation of information, for it exploited a range of media, such as video and pictures, and promoted different approaches to the written word. Text can be presented in different ways, using captions – for example – or pop ups, and we have seen an example of this in the previous chapter where we discussed the potential of Wordle as a means of developing expressive vocabulary. Text, or rather hypertext, is also more interactive and can be more easily integrated and juxtaposed with other media.

This is of particular benefit to children who do not like to engage with traditional texts and provides a different tool to the practitioner to entice disaffected readers to interact creatively with text. However, it does not limit the more able reader who can find stimulating and challenging opportunities in the same environment. It could be suggested that the blog or wiki can offer the same type of appeal for developing writing.

Composing a blog can be very stimulating as children not only communicate through the written word, but also by the use of pictures and hyperlinks. Some children find this appealing and this form of presentation may help to take the 'hard work' out of writing. It may offer an attractive alternative to a blank page of an exercise book, which can be intimidating. What is more, the wider context provided by blogging on the web can give impetus to write. The subject or focus of many blogs would be considered non-academic, addressing pedestrian themes like favourite hobbies or pastimes. Many children's first attempts at creating blogs involve similar themes and might typically describe hobbies like football or favourite books, comics or television programmes. In the production of these blogs, children will be very engaged because they can be seen to be developing and extending an existing body of literature. In doing so, they are writing regularly and are given a vehicle for their 'voice', which provides an outlet for their own enthusiasms.

Blogs can therefore be viewed as accessible and non-threatening and act as a reflection of the author's developing personality. What is more, the blog offers a mechanism to write instantaneously and in a way that makes it easy to edit previous compositions. Meanwhile, the ability to include different types of colour and media add further multimodal interest. Blogging in school also provides a form of writing that increasingly matches the way that children, teenagers and adults choose to communicate out of school hours. The blurring of the boundary between educational and social communication might be seen to engage a young audience and provides an opportunity to establish standards in terms of writing and language that can influence broader patterns of communication.

During the composition of blogs, children will be experiencing a great deal of supplementary learning. While a blog might not be associated with a 'traditional' literacy lesson, children are still confronting issues like the structure of writing, the application of punctuation and the appeal of the language incorporated in the composition. In this respect the prospect of a wider audience increases motivation and, of course, the time spent reading, interpreting and evaluating the blogs created by other class members, offers a wealth of learning opportunities.

Davies and Merchant (2009) discuss the fact that blogs need to be seen as more than free standing constructs. To make meaning from blogs, the user will read across a range of examples and in creating their own should seek to identify and develop links to other web documents, via 'suggested links' perhaps of embedded hypertext. These authors conclude that blogs need to be read and understood as part of a wider network of texts (Davies and Merchant 2009: 82) and while we have already seen that this can enhance motivation, it is worth considering the additional benefits in terms of digital literacy.

This cross-blog construction of meaning requires children to engage in a different approach to reading than that required by a linear text. It will certainly require them to track themes and make connections between the various sources they are using. Even if children are not reading blogs across the web as described above – and there are safety issues to account for – they can do this in a similar but more restricted way and within a smaller-scale environment using the school's own facilities. Children might be involved in reading across blogs and making connections to those produced by the community of the school, for example, using a VLE or e-portfolio tool.

Another feature of working with blogs and wikis is that they encourage reflection. They could, therefore, offer potential engagement with higher levels of learning. A blog captures the development of a thought process and therefore encourages the author to reflect upon that process as well as the subject in hand. In addition each blog post tends to be the culmination of a process in which the blog owner reflects over and ponders on themes that are to be discussed. This consideration of issues will usually occur while contributing to the blog, but it will also continue to play out in the mind's eye of the author at various points in the day, when relevant ideas will be identified and tentatively played with. The evaluation of substance and the continual, ongoing thought processes that occur when keeping a blog surely encourages children to be more reflective.

As previously discussed in Section 1 of this book, Web 2.0 tools like blogs and wikis provide the opportunity to publish work to a wider audience than that offered by traditional classroom writing exercises. These tools have a feature that allows comments to be left on entries by the consumers of the material. Peer evaluation made up of both written comments and maybe even recorded comments that are then uploaded to the blog or wiki can further contribute to the reflective process. This collaborative approach should be seen as an important part of scaffolding the learning process. Learning in this fashion becomes a widening and collectively broader experience of 'we think' or 'we all learn' rather than an individualized task of what 'I think' or 'I learn' (Selwyn 2011: 76).

It has been noted that keeping and maintaining a blog, or creating a wiki, forces children to write regularly and repetitively. It cannot be overlooked that this repeated engagement with text can only give children increased practice when expressing their thoughts and for this reason alone they should remain a feature of the classroom and not be considered a passing phase. For some children, but not all, this might present the 'best' way to communicate. Just as 'electronic texts' should be included as part of all the different types of reading material that are offered to a class, blogs and wikis must therefore make up one of the ways children seek to express their thoughts.

For some children, the use of blogs has resulted in raising their overall attainment in literacy; their results may not have been so noticeable had they not been able to use this tool. Garner (2011) comments on schools that have used blogging as a means to get boys to write, reporting that the use of blogs resulted in Year 6 boys creating stories of 5,000 words in length. This helped to take the school's level 5 achievement in SATS from 7 per cent to 63 per cent – a significant improvement. Davis and Merchant (2009: 82) state that blogging in schools should be considered a highly desirable activity and that educators should ensure they bring these texts into the classroom.

As well as using Web 2.0 tools like blogs and wikis for educational purposes with children, they also offer an opportunity for professional development for teachers. There is now a whole range of blogs that are created by educators that act as a means by which teachers can extend their professional knowledge. Teachers will create blogs that may discuss specialist knowledge in one particular curriculum area. For instance, the subject of ICT is the mainstay of many blogs made by teachers for teachers. Other blogs will serve as a conduit to an array of fruitful sites on a certain theme.

Engagement with Web 2.0 on this level might also serve another purpose. Carrington (2009) notes that the way in which teachers interact with the world outside the classroom will influence their classroom practice. The effective use of resources like wikis and the development of attitudes and skills that culminate in the notion of a 'participatory culture' will become more prominent in the classroom if teachers are engaging in digital technology in order to conduct both their social engagement and professional development. She also relates the use of technology to the work of Jenkins (2006) to propose that teachers should take note of a 'hidden curriculum' of participation that is offered to both the work place and social scenarios. She advocates that teachers should be considering how to experiment with and mix media and cultural content, work collaboratively across a range of contexts, evaluate and synthesise information as well as adopting different identities and stances. If teachers are to understand and relate to young people they need to be aware of the features of the social landscape of their subjects.

Practical Task

- As a practitioner begin to immerse yourself in blogs. A good place to start in order to familiarise yourself with them is at this site: http://edublogawards.com/ In addition, look at http://primaryweb2.wikispaces.com/blogs to view a variety of blogs made by children in schools in various parts of the globe.
- If you are using blogs with children it is beneficial to spend a little time concentrating on the format and layout of blogs so that they know and understand the characteristics of them.
- Ask children to consider the different array of blogs available.
- Examine with children the different ways you might read and 'make meaning from a blog'.

- Consider how to encourage children to critically evaluate blogs. What do they need to know about the integrity and validity of different blogs?
- Are there any e-safety issues to be considered when reading blogs across the World Wide Web.
- When initially starting to blog with children make sure that you are proactive at leaving comments on their work. This will encourage them to come back to their blog and add to it. Feedback is as important on a blog as it is in an exercise book. Not commenting on a blog could be equated to leaving a piece of work unmarked.

Case study 1: use of a wiki (exploring the solar system)

Year 6 were investigating the 'the Earth and beyond' using wikis to help them in their exploration. The class were new to this technology as a form of communication so their teacher started the learning with a simple task. The class teacher created a wiki on the school's VLE. He initially populated the wiki with some information on The Moon. He encouraged his class to contribute to, and extend the wiki by asking them to research a feature of the solar system and then recording the information on it. The class were required to do this as part of their homework tasks. Gradually, the children started to add detail and build up a collection of information or, as described by the teacher, a 'database' of information.

This approach was adopted in order to provide the children with a simple introduction to the tools and principles associated with the wiki. They were required to access the page frequently in order to make simple updates, which familiarised them with the processes and the teacher was able to make encouraging comments on the wiki, stimulating participation. He also printed the information out and shared it with the class in order to give another form of motivation to other children who were yet to access the technology. This demonstrated that the teacher valued the efforts of the children and, once a good body of information had been added to the wiki, he was able to discuss the value of using this kind of tool to share work with the whole class. This also provided a good opportunity to discuss similar World Wide Web applications like Wikipedia, encouraging the children to understand the advantages and disadvantages of this type of user produced resource as a means of obtaining knowledge.

Feeling satisfied that the children had made a good start with the use of wikis the teacher then moved away from this type of technology for a couple of weeks with a view to returning to it. He did this deliberately in order to let the class digest and reflect on new ways of working. In the meantime the class continued with their exploration of the solar system in a practical activity that required the children to design and make an 'imaginary planet'. The children had to decide on the features of a new planet which included, among other considerations, physical relief of the land, the type of atmosphere, temperature levels, hours of daylight, proximity to the sun and types of life that such an environment might sustain. The children were also given the opportunity to create a likeness of their planet using a balloon and papier mâché, finished with the application of various materials.

Once the class had finished the practical expression of this topic, the teacher once again returned to the wiki, this time for a more demanding purpose. Each child was assigned their own page on the wiki and used it to record details of their imaginary planet. This time, although the teacher continued to provide feedback on the thoughts of his class, the children were asked to explore the pages of other children and to comment. In this way, the children were able to find out about different ideas as well as leaving comments for their peers to think about. In their comments, some children encouraged others to consider the sustainability of their planets, if the conditions on the planet appeared hostile to life, for example. In this way, the class was encouraged to consider the practicalities of their ideas and the children were required to evaluate their design and to make changes in order to improve the viability of their suggestions.

Overall, the teacher felt that the project was successful and offered certain advantages over more traditional approaches. He felt that the children could have easily recorded their ideas in their exercise books, but concluded that this might not have given the same impetus to improve their work. The children would have spent much time recording their ideas using pencil and paper and, once they handed the work in, would have viewed that to be the final stage of the exercise. Improvements that might be suggested would be seen as a 'chore' and subsequently reluctantly applied. Instead, the wiki provided a context in which improvements were very easily implemented. Moreover, as the improvements had been offered by their peers as a form of assessing each other, the teacher felt that better levels of reflection and evaluation were encouraged.

In addition to this, the teacher felt that the use of the wiki encouraged the children to be more creative. Looking through the wiki and reading the ideas of others had stimulated children to consider, and then add, additional features to their own planet. He also observed that the wiki enabled children to access this project both in class and while at home. Some had particularly enjoyed this type of writing in the class and the teacher observed that concentration levels were easier to engage and maintain.

The authors are grateful to C. Gayle, Year 6 teacher at Kingsham Primary School West Sussex.

Case study 2: blogging (fictional diaries)

Year 6 had been studying World War II; in particular they had been looking at the diary of Anne Frank. The children had read some of the text written by Anne Frank and they had also watched the film inspired by her story. The children had spent time discussing the plight of this child and the restricted conditions in which she had lived. The class had explored why, when living in such cramped and challenging conditions, the diary of Anne Frank might have acted as a form of escape for her and a mechanism by which she could express feelings and thoughts, that she might not otherwise have had opportunity to articulate. The diary might also have given her a form of privacy and something that was special to her alone in a situation that forced her to share all other parts of her life.

Using the diary as a stimulus, the teacher of this class asked the children to recreate a diary in the spirit of Anne Frank. They were asked to imagine that they were in a similar plight, which resulted in their living in restricted and dangerous situations, but in 2010; here the teacher was giving a modern day slant on this situation. The class were able to select the way they chose to present their ideas. They could either produce their work using traditional means – in the form of a diary by making entries in their literacy books, or they could present their thoughts using a blog.

For those children who chose to use a blog the teacher found there to be certain advantages. Some children were more motivated to write using an electronic form of communication rather than a diary and there were organisational benefits because the presentation of the blog meant that all the thoughts of the child were in one place. As a result, it was easy for the children to track and trace the development of their thoughts and read back through their entries. Those who were not using the blog did not find this kind of tracking quite as simple as they had recorded their thoughts in their literacy books and their entries had become interspersed with other pieces of writing, completed during other lessons.

The blog, like the wikis discussed above, also provided the opportunity for both the teacher and peers to leave comments, expressing what they liked about the blog and what needed to be improved. The teacher also found that the children were more considerate in inserting correct punctuation in the text. He felt that, because the children could not touch type, they were slower in the process of communication and this actually made them more particular in their application of themes like the capitalisation of letters and full stops. This is surprising in light of comments by authors like Palmer, who speak of electronic communication speeding up the brain to the detriment of learning (Palmer 2006). In contrast, he felt that when using pen and paper children became very automatic in their method of communication and that this made them less likely to punctuate accurately and thoroughly.

The use of blogs and traditional diaries also brought another dimension to the learning. The class were able to consider themes associated with 'e-safety'. The pupils discussed how, with diaries, the audience for that text is usually only one person, unless it is accidentally discovered by another or purposefully shared by the owner. Indeed, with some diaries, the user can actually physically lock them. In comparison, although a 'web-log' often takes the form of a diary, the audience for this text is not one person, but potentially anyone who can access the World Wide Web. As such, the class considered the different ways the population of the twenty-first century communicated.

This provided the teacher with an opportunity to reinforce the fact that, when using a blog, the children could potentially share information with other writers and as a result the 'e-safety' code should always be applied. He reminded the children that they should only use their first name and never give out any private information when writing. In this case, the blogs produced by the children were published within the relative security of the school's virtual learning platform and were therefore only available to people who had the password to access the site. Nevertheless, the lesson in e-safety remained paramount as the class were required to realise that it was not just pupils who could access the blog but the whole school community, which could consist of a few hundred people including adults. Finally, the class considered the changes in the way people spread news. They considered that if Anne Frank had lived in the present day she just might have been able to make her plight known to a wider audience who might have been able to help her through the mechanism of the World Wide Web.

The authors are grateful to C. Gayle of Kingsham Primary School, West Sussex for the inspiration for this idea.

Case study 3: brainstorming and organising thoughts

Tool focus

Wallwisher (http://www.wallwisher.com)

Wallwisher is an application that builds on the concept of Post-it notes. This program allows you to make 'virtual sticky notes' and add them to a virtual wall. As such, it provides a good way to collect information quickly from a class and present ideas in an appealing manner. Wallwisher offers an alternative solution to Post it notes that are often used in class, but difficult to store in an organised fashion. They are liable to get lost or have the frustrating habit of losing their adhesiveness and then repeatedly falling off. More importantly, however, Wallwisher is another Web 2.0 tool that encourages children to collaborate and communicate.

Wallwisher is relatively easy to use and is free. Potential wall builders only have to register before being able to create a wall for themselves. When making a wall, users are offered the opportunity to consider privacy rights and choose between options limiting who can view and contribute posts. There is also the additional option of the 'owner' of the wall being able to view and moderate all posts before allowing them to be placed on the virtual wall. This important facility provides an added level of security if the wall being created has been configured to be available to all potential Wallwisher users.

A wall is built by giving it a name and by selecting a suitable background. Once that has been carried out, sticky notes can be added simply by double clicking on the wall. When adding a new note you will get the option of adding text to the wall or adding pictures, audio files or even YouTube clips by simply copying and pasting in a URL or, in the case of video, the embed code. Users of YouTube should be aware that the 'new' embed code is not compatible with all platforms and, if problems occur, try using the 'old code', which can be accessed by selecting the relevant option on the YouTube page. Generally speaking, the chances of success of adding additional multimedia information can be variable. At times, when adding pictures, the user will get a symbol that enables them to view the information only when doubled clicked (see the example in the screen shot). At other times a pasted URL will result in the actual material being displayed on the wall itself. Users often utilise collections of graphics offered by facilities like 'Google images' when copying and pasting media to walls and practitioners do have to be wary of copyright laws.

When creating sticky notes there is a 160 character limit for each. Sticky notes can be moved around the wall if that person has created the note itself; a contributor cannot move the notes of others, although the overall 'owner' of the wall has the facility to move all the notes that appear on it. Notes can be edited at a later date should this be desired. Finally there is a very useful blog that accompanies Wallwisher that discusses changes to, and new features of this program.

Year 5 were starting the topic of World War II. Valuing an 'enquiry' approach to learning, the class teacher wanted the children to raise some of the questions for the topic instead of dictating what the content of the learning journey should be. She also wanted to find out what kind of information the children already knew about this period of history. Needing a tool where the ideas of the children could be easily displayed, the teacher decided that Wallwisher would be a suitable program for this type of approach. During their first lesson the teacher introduced the topic by reading the class a short story that was written from the point of view of a child in the war. She also showed the pupils images of children in the war using the BBC website on primary history (http://www.bbc.co.uk/schools/primaryhistory/world_war2/).

Next, the teacher asked the children to work in small groups in order to pool their ideas on World War II. She also required them to select one piece of information relating to that subject that they would like to discover. The teacher then used Wallwisher to display the thoughts of the class and the children made sticky notes to record the information they had discussed in groups and the subjects that they wanted to explore next. The teacher then sorted the sticky notes so that one side of the wall illustrated the known information, while future directions were posted on the other side. In this manner the teacher created a very durable and lasting record of what the children had discussed and also produced a display of the questions the children wished to find out more about, thereby letting them have a stake in the direction of the learning for the term.

The above is just one very simple example of how Wallwisher can be used in class. The communicative nature of this program means that it could also act as a useful vehicle for a variety of other learning tasks. For instance, it would be a very good mechanism to record information when children are studying sentence level work in literacy lessons and where children might be thinking about extending their expressive vocabulary.

As an example of this, consider lessons that might require children to construct alternative words for overused terms like 'nice' or 'said'. The teacher might provide a starter sentence on a virtual wall that contained a dull sentence like: 'Katie thought her

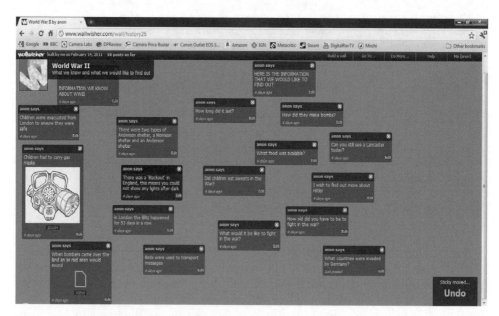

Figure 7.1 Wallwisher: sorting the knowns from the known unknowns

ice-cream was nice'. Children would then create virtual notes, which contained the same sentence, but using a more stimulating word than 'nice' in order to finish the sentence. If the children had access to laptops or PCs they could each contribute sticky notes in a class-collaboration on this theme. The resulting wall displayed on an Inter-active Whiteboard at the front of the class would then act as a stimulus for children for the duration of the remainder of the lesson.

Alternatively Wallwisher could act as a useful resource in which children could show their understanding of a certain concept that had been learnt previously. For instance, it is very easy to find numerous examples of walls showing understanding of mathe-matical concepts – this includes walls that have been made by children to show their own conceptual knowledge and understanding, as well as walls that have been created by teachers to help students.

Case study 4: use of wikis and VLE forums (teaching the Egyptians)

In the following case study wikis are once again used to encourage 'anytime' learning. However, in this example the teacher uses a combination of online features typically offered by a VLE to help to deliver his lessons.

Year 5 was learning about the ancient Egyptians and the teacher was keen to use online tools with his class. As in the first case study in this chapter, the class were fairly new to this sort of technology and, again, the teacher gave the children the simple task of looking at Wikipedia. On doing so the class discussed who had produced this site and they were actually extremely surprised to discover that it had not been produced by a 'company'. The fact that the expansion of this site depended entirely on users adding content and the fact that different contributors could edit and amend informa-tion was a new concept to them.

The next stage in the exercise involved the pupils exploring the theme of Egyptian gods. The teacher created a wiki front page and placed one god on it with some accompanying information detailing the nature and function of the god. Using the internet, the children were then required to research an Egyptian god of their own choice and then add their information to their own wiki page. The teacher also dis-cussed with the children the navigation around the wiki site and how to structure links between pages. The teacher helped the children with their web quest to find out about gods by selecting and placing suitable links on a forum, which the children accessed via the Moodle VLE.

Having introduced this technology to the children, the teacher was then happy to use the collaborative opportunities offered by the VLE to encourage online communication during a homework task. The teacher wanted to move away from the more passive, research aspect of the topic and introduce work that would continue the active discus-sion he had encouraged in class. To achieve this, the teacher continued to populate the Egyptian forum. He found a picture of an Egyptian tomb painting with part of it missing and placed it on the forum and asked the children to study the painting as a homework task. They were then required to place entries on the forum so that they could suggest what was happening in the painting, to make deductions about Egyptian life from the image and also to propose what might have been happening in the missing part of the image. The teacher designed this activity so that children would be required to hypothesise, predict, enquire and question.

Initially, when using the forum the teacher monitored the activity on it quite closely. At the start of the exercise, the novelty of this sort of communication resulted in the class using it in a way in which the teacher had not originally envisaged. The children made the most of the opportunity to 'chat' online and they contacted each other with conversational messages rather than considering the task at hand. The teacher allowed this to happen for a short period, but then encouraged the children to concentrate their messages on Egyptians by posting constructive comments on the forum. Every time a child posted a valuable thought he made certain to reply. He also monitored the conversation closely in order that his comments modelled the type of language and online etiquette that they should adhere to.

Fairly quickly, the children started to focus their thoughts. Reflecting on this part of the learning, the teacher concluded that he found the technology effective in allowing the children to bounce ideas off each other. He established that the teaching strategy added to the thought process of the children as peer and teacher led responses to posts encouraged them to consider new ideas, thoughts that they had previously not realised, and helped them to move on in their understanding.

To continue to encourage the children to contribute to the forum and to maintain the momentum of this type of learning, the teacher used the VLE to create a glossary on the ancient Egyptians. Every time the children came across a new item of vocabulary they entered it into the glossary and produced a definition to accompany it. In this way, the children were able to extend their working subject knowledge of this period of history. The teacher also encouraged the children to sustain their interest in the glossary by using a feature of the VLE to add a fun dimension to the learning. Using the game of online 'hangman' the VLE was set up to show the definition of a word in the glossary. The children then had to guess the word while playing hangman. The children were given six guesses in order to work out the word or they lost the game.

The authors are grateful to P. Aldren, Midhurst Primary School, West Sussex for the inspiration for this idea.

Conclusion

In an earlier chapter we described a distinct category of technology that was relevant to this discussion, but was not so immediately applicable to the kind of classroom activities encountered in this section so far. In some cases, this is because the technologies are new and are only gradually developing to a point that would make them usable in a classroom environment. In this category we might include the social bookmarking tools and even the really simple syndication services that were described in the opening chapters of this book. In other cases, this is because they perform a function that means that they would not necessarily be used by children in the independent and creative ways that we have emphasised so far. These might include virtual learning environments like Moodle, which incorporate the functionality of social software like blogs and wikis, but are otherwise part of the learning environment provided by the school and are not tools in the hands of the children themselves.

However, teachers need to view these technologies as being relevant to their professional development. Over time they are likely to become more useable and it is important to reflect on how the digital literacy of children is improving all the time. This means that they might acquire a function within classroom activities in the future. At the same time, some tools can be used by teachers to enhance their own practice and to add a new dimension to their teaching. We will therefore address these technologies within this concluding chapter of the section.

We have seen that virtual learning environments (VLEs) have been introduced into schools as part of the drive towards personalisation. They are seen to offer flexibility to the child, who is able to use them to bridge the worlds of home and class and to share work with parents and other people from outside school. They are also seen to extend the learning environment in ways that reflect better the varied needs of learners, not all of whom find it easy to express themselves in traditional environments, and to provide teachers with a means of working closely with individual children. In these ways and others, the virtual learning environment is seen as a means of promoting an approach to schooling that tailors learning to the needs of the individual child.

The simplest way to think of a VLE is as a website. You access it through a standard web browser and once you have done so, you quickly realise that you are really just navigating through a series of web pages and web based tools. The difference between the VLE and websites that you are accustomed to using in a more day to day context is that the VLE is designed to be organised and customised by users whose areas of expertise lie in fields other than web development and design. In this sense then, they can be considered Web 2.0 tools and much of what happens within a VLE is mediated by the same kinds of technology that we have referred to in connection with blogs and wikis. There are differences. VLEs typically offer lots of control over the appearance and organisation of pages as well as tools that allow content to be added or created on the page. However, assuming that you are now familiar with Web 2.0 tools you should find that you are familiar with many aspects of the environment.

Taking a less mechanistic approach, Weller (2007: 5) defines the virtual learning environment as a 'software system that combines a number of different tools that are used to systematically deliver content online and facilitate the learning experience around that content'. As a definition it is necessarily vague as different virtual learning environments are quite varied. However, it captures the essential ingredients that they have in common. All VLEs allow educators to store materials and resources and to make these available selectively, so that the individual child sees only those materials that are relevant to them. These materials can be organised so as reflect the structure of the curriculum and, within that framework, of a project, a scheme of work or even an individual lesson. These materials can then be browsed, scrutinised and downloaded from any computer that has access to the internet, providing the user has a valid username and password.

In addition to this, VLEs typically offer tools that allow users to communicate with one another and to create their own content. Communication tools are normally categorised as being synchronous, like chat facilities, which support real time communication, and asynchronous, like discussion boards, which allow users to contribute at a time and at a pace that suits them. However, these distinctions are easily blurred. For example, discussion boards can be used by multiple users simultaneously and all the tools can be used in a wide variety of ways, depending upon the context. A discussion board can be used to conduct an open discussion, but might equally support a more structured process of interaction – such as a question and answer session – or simply serve as a mechanism for submitting work online. This is possible because file attachments can normally be added to discussion board posts. Using these tools effectively requires teachers to think imaginatively about the ways that dialogue can promote learning in a given context and to select the best tool and the best approach to using that tool.

In the same spirit, users need to take an adaptable and creative approach to the tools that allow students to create content. We do not have to dwell on these as we have addressed most of them in the preceding chapters. They are simply versions of the social software that we encountered under the headings of blogs and wikis. However, the fact that they are brought together into a single environment that places them alongside structured resources and communication tools does create some significant opportunities. As Weller says, the purpose of the environment is to facilitate the learning process around resources and it falls to the teacher to think about how these tools might function in combination with each other, within an integrated learning environment. Many of the case studies in this section have exemplified this principle, but it is useful for the teacher to start by looking at the combination of tools available to them in their own VLE.

Practical task

Identify all the tools that support communication and content creation on the VLE that you use at college or at school. Access any of them that you have not already used and explore any tools that you can access that allow you to adapt their configuration. For example, are you able to set up blogs in ways that allow authors to keep their posts private from one another and can you control who can comment? Equally, can you create wikis for specific groups of children or that only allow people to edit them at specified times? You may need to ask for help as these options are sometimes considered quite advanced. However, this can be a useful exercise in itself.

Apart from anything else the ability to operate fluidly between different online environments and to marshal different online tools for a single purpose is an important element of digital literacy. However, this kind of exercise requires a particular form of planning on the part of the teacher, who must understand how to combine and inter-link the various tools that the children need to use within the broader virtual learning environment. This is why it is important to consider these tools under the heading of pro-fessional issues. Can links to dedicated blogs or to specially created wiki pages be inserted alongside learning materials and resources or can the resources be delivered through the social software tools themselves? These are important issues for the teacher to explore.

Another system that is beginning to be introduced in schools and shares many characteristics with the VLE is the e-portfolio. Both are effectively online software tools and both can be accessed from any internet connection as a result. Both require users to provide passwords in order to access the full array of services and tools and both consist fundamentally of web pages and web tools connected by hyperlinks and grouped together into little 'mini-web-sites'. However, where the VLE is oriented towards the needs of the teacher the e-portfolio is much more learner centred.

On a VLE, the teacher tends to have control and finds tools that allow her to recre-ate a space that feels a little like the classroom. It is created by the teacher for one thing, and all the children come there in order to receive materials or instructions or to participate in prescribed tasks. Their work might come to acquire a significant profile with in the learning environment, but it is the teacher who sets the stage and the teacher who retains ultimate control.

On an e-portfolio, on the other hand, the users have a personal space that they can customise, in terms of presentation, organise and share as they please. This freedom can normally be limited at an administrator level, so teachers can be given access to all areas, for example, but schools are naturally more cautious about this kind of tech-nology because it appears to undermine the primacy of the teacher within the learning environment. Questions may be asked about whether children are competent to main-tain their own portfolios and it is certainly true to say that we are far from that situa-tion where we would expect to see these kinds of tools being used on a regular basis.

Nevertheless, as we have already seen, it is important to be alert to the increasing level of digital literacy among children and the early inroads of e-portfolios into schools suggest that they might become a tool of the future. For example in New Hampshire (USA) it has been a requirement for the last five years that all children have an e-portfolio page by the eighth grade (NHED 2005) and these tools are now quite routinely used from the earliest age groups (Bolduc and Gonzalez 2010). It is, therefore, important for teachers to consider them as something of interest and they are important for us to consider in this discussion.

The motivation to use the e-portfolio is similar to that of the VLE in so far as it appears to offer a way of extending the learning environment in a manner conducive to personalisation. In fact one might argue that this system offers a more direct route to this objective. On an e-portfolio the child occupies their own private space and is therefore able to showcase work and conduct dialogue with individuals within this environment. On a VLE this situation has to be contrived as the space is, by default, public, albeit within a strictly defined group. However, we might go further than this simple observation.

In a previous chapter we looked at the enthusiasm that many people, young people included, displayed for social networking sites. We observed that there were serious issues about using social networking tools in an educational environment – particularly in a primary education context – and commented on the emphatically recreational nature of networks like club penguin, Moshimonsters and even Facebook. However, we speculated then that there might be lessons that we could draw from the popularity of social networking and that these were likely to centre on the enthusiasm with which people went about creating profiles and exploring identity within an online environment. The debate about personalisation throws some new light on this discussion, as it is closely tied up with the learning of the individual child.

Personalisation in its present form may not retain its current, very prominent place within the educational agenda. We have seen that recent political changes have created an uncertain future for many policy areas within the field of education and that some practitioners have expressed serious doubts about the viability of personalisation as a policy direction. Nevertheless it appears that the broader principle, that education should be more sensitive and more responsive to the needs and preferences of the individual child is likely to play a part in educational thinking in the future. This being the case, the e-portfolio becomes a tool that is likely to emerge as a feature of the learning environment as it emphasises the importance of the individual by giving them greater scope to develop a sense of individual identity through the development of an online profile.

In this sense then, the e-portfolio performs a function similar to that of the social networking site, which allows the user to shrug off the anonymity imposed by the World Wide Web and develop an individual identity. However, unlike sites like Facebook, which encourage one to establish an identity as a social being, the e-portfolio emphasises the characteristics relevant to the individual's identity as a learner. While the e-portfolio allows users to do many things that people do on social networking sites, uploading photographs for example and embedding favourite bits of video, the essential components of the e-portfolio are more akin to the virtual learning environment, consisting of folders for files, blogs, RSS feeds and lists of hyperlinks or 'bookmarks'. The e-portfolio is, to state the matter bluntly, a virtual learning environment centred on the child as a learner.

Again, the challenge for the teacher lies not so much in knowing how to use any given tool on the e-portfolio, but in identifying the ways in which the environment itself, as defined by the combination of these tools, can be used constructively. For example, one of the great strengths of the e-portfolio that is already being exploited derives from the way that the system preserves the ongoing learning process for each individual child.

In a project run in elementary schools from the Oyster River Cooperative School District in New Hampshire (Bolduc and Gonzalez 2010) e-portfolios were used to, among other things: 'help students become more reflective about themselves as learners ... To help teachers learn about their students [and] ... To help students see technology as a tool to be used for a different purpose (creating a portfolio) rather than an end to itself' (ORCSD 2010). Children started at kindergarten stage, where they were videoed by teachers discussing what they wanted to be in later life. At this stage interaction with the e-portfolio was mediated by the teacher, but the children were introduced to the concept and the fact that they would be able to look back at this when they were seniors. By first grade they were scanning writing and putting this kind of work on the e-portfolio themselves and did so at three points in the year, demonstrating progress, and by third grade were writing book reports directly on to the portfolio itself.

By doing this, children were invited to consider and reflect upon their progress, while teachers across the district were able to compare the work of children in different classes and evaluate the effectiveness of different practices. What is more, the portfolio was a space, where teachers and children were able to conduct a private, two-way conversation about their work and the personal interests that underpinned this work. This aspect of the tools has been explored in the UK, where the personalisation agenda promotes a focus on the progress and needs of individual children. FutureLab make the link between personalisation and reflection in this way: 'In order for learners to control their own personalised learning they need to truly understand their own needs' (FutureLab 2007: 19). Crossley Heath School in Halifax can be seen to have acknowledged this in the design of their VLE, where they selected a learning platform that facilitates the creation of individual 'homepages' for students (Lees 2009). The product that they used, Frog, is a sophisticated online tool that encompasses the functionality of a VLE and an e-portfolio and allowed pupils and teachers to communicate via personal pages. This was well received by pupils, one of whom reported that: 'we definitely feel that we are being listened to. That makes us want to contribute to the VLE' (ibid. 2009: 57).

Nevertheless, despite these very positive beginnings we are still at an early stage in our development of educational applications for e-portfolios, particularly in the primary phase. One of the issues that teachers encounter with this type of facility is that, with the exception of the blog, many of the tools contained within the e-portfolio are rather less familiar than those used routinely in the VLE. For example, these include RSS and the facility to embed content from media sharing sites like YouTube and Flickr. While we have discussed these tools it must be acknowledged that it is harder to conceive of them playing a central role within classroom activities. In order to understand their potential as tools within an integrated digital learning environment we must consider their functionality in more detail.

Take the case of RSS or Really Simple Syndication. Within an e-portfolio an adult user might use the RSS facility to create a channel to a favourite blog. This might be a blog that they maintain for a wider audience, meaning that work they do in one context does not need to be duplicated in another. Alternatively the blog might be authored by another person, in which case the RSS feed is being used in order to create a dynamic link to a completely independent source of content on the World Wide Web. Actually in this case we need not limit ourselves to considering blogs as many other types of websites offer feeds of this sort. A portfolio owner might choose to create a feed to a site like the national archives homepage, so that they could be notified about the availability of new archive materials as these were released into the public domain.

Alternatively they might start a feed from a popular news site like the BBC (http://www.bbc.co.uk) or the *Guardian* (http://www.guardian.co.uk) ensuring that headlines were channelled directly to their portfolio as they were published on the web. In fact, several feeds of this sort could be placed upon a page within a portfolio, creating a hub where internet content of different types and from different sources is consolidated.

One could possibly envisage how primary aged children might use e-portfolios in equivalent ways. Children friendly news sites like Newsround maintain RSS feeds and there are a range of websites producing educational information on a variety of subjects that are appropriate for children, which can be linked in this way (e.g. http://www.weeklyreader.com or http://www.sciencenewsforkids.org). Returning to the notion of linking to blogs, it is possible to envisage how the e-portfolio could become a hub where a range of classroom activities involving blogs could be consolidated.

The ability to embed content from media sharing sites offers a means of extending this principle to a wide range of resources that children may have created in activities similar to those described in the preceding case studies and classroom ideas. Examples might include podcasts, submitted to YouTube or Teacher Tube, Glogs and even Myebook creations, although the user may be obliged to limit themselves to providing hyperlinks in some of these cases. This allows the results of these kinds of classroom activities to be presented alongside other types of work that the child might display in their portfolio.

The ability to create RSS feeds and to embed content from other sites creates an additional dimension to the e-portfolio therefore; we do not need not see it as an isolated space on the web, where a personalised perspective on learning can be created, but as a place where the individual user can create a personalised view of the internet as well. This recalls earlier discussion about RSS and social bookmarking, in relation to wider considerations about the usefulness of the internet as a learning environment. At that point, we noted that searches of the web via search engines like Google can be disorienting and misleading for learners. We saw that the results are often unsatisfactory from the point of view of the teacher and the student and that tools that allowed more structured approaches to interaction with the internet were required.

Given discussion in this and previous chapters, it is possible to see how VLEs and e-portfolios could develop in order to serve this need. Staying with the e-portfolio for a moment, we could envisage how a teacher might use their own portfolio pages to provide windows on relevant parts of the web. They might use it to mount and juxtapose material that they have discovered in their own research or to make trusted sites available to children for their own independent study. In doing so they provide an environment in which it is easier for children to access materials and to refer between them. It also deals with a number of issues around e-safety as it reduces the likelihood that inappropriate material will be encountered accidentally in the course of web navigation.

Of course, an argument against this course of action is that children become 'over protected' and are not exposed to experiences that improve their digital literacy. However, although this could follow from an overly prescriptive application of the principles outlined above, the desire to enhance the digital literacy of children provides a powerful incentive to use tools like RSS and environments like the e-portfolio. Not only is the RSS tool itself an important feature of advanced web use, its use by children positively encourages them to engage with key issues. For example, it promotes their understanding of the way in which the web environment functions and encourages them to consider the nature of different online contexts. By creating a feed to a specific piece of content the child is creating a new context for a resource that has been created in another. They are invited to consider how the original context for the material they selected relates to other features of their learning environment and how their learning relates to wider patterns of social and cultural life.

Of course, digital literacy is a very important theme within this discussion and it invites us to consider the other tool that we have not addressed so far and that is social bookmarking. Again the attraction of social bookmarking is that it helps to provide structure to children's use of the internet and again it is easy to envisage how a teacher could assemble a list of bookmarks that identifies useful and trusted sites for children to use and makes them accessible in a safe way. However, the real potential for social bookmarking will doubtless only be realised when it becomes a tool in the hands of the children themselves.

The key feature of the social bookmarking site and of the process of bookmarking the internet in a social environment is that children are encouraged to annotate their links with a potential audience in mind. In doing so they are encouraged to perform the exact same steps that we want children to go through in their day to day evaluation of web content. As we have seen, they are required to create 'tags' that define the purpose and the context of the site. This means that other users are more likely to find this site as a result of keyword searches and children are encouraged to think about the ways in which sites could be classified.

In addition to this bookmarks should be annotated with comments that bear upon the quality of the content. Again, this involves applying many of the critical and analytical criteria that we hope that children will be aware of as discriminating users of web content. While bookmarking a single website is unlikely to have much impact in terms of digital literacy, if bookmarking, tagging and annotating websites becomes a routine part of classroom interaction with the internet, the children will not only be developing a substantial and searchable resource for their own studies, but will also be developing important skills.

At this point it is necessary to draw this book to a close. The look of the classroom of tomorrow is not a clear one. At present, even the nature of the curriculum for the learners of the near future has not been decided. What is more certain is that the children we teach today, the adults of our future, will need to be technologically aware in order for them to be able to participate in social, cultural, financial and even political matters. Children need to be able to access the World Wide Web in a knowledgeable and safe manner. Schools should teach children to be digitally literate and equip them with the skills of critical analysis in order that they can peruse the wealth of information available to them on the web in a discerning manner. For the twenty-first-century learner, knowledge is now easy to come by and a cheap commodity. Children need to be equipped by schools with the skills and understanding of how to put that knowledge to good use.

Web 2.0 tools, the subject of this text, are diverse, interchanging and numerous in nature. Used in the right way they provide a wealth of learning opportunities. Feynman (1999), theoretical physicist, Nobel Prize winner and arguably one of the century's most brilliant thinkers, discusses his 'pleasure of finding things out'. He talks of his enjoyment of a 'playful' approach to learning, of finding things out simply for the 'fun' of it.

This view of learning can be compared to many of the experiences of Web 2.0 learning; this type of technology allows children to explore in a playful manner. Children most probably initially meet Web 2.0 in a recreational environment and associate forms of this type of technology with pleasure. Schools need to recognise this and harness the potential of social software for educational outcomes. In addition, it could be suggested that educators are currently preparing students for jobs that do not yet exist, using technologies that have yet to be invented in order to solve problems that we do not even know are problems yet (Fisch and McLeod 2007). This argument alone should reinforce the notion that the place of Web 2.0 should be integral to the make-up of the primary classroom.

References

Abs, P. et al. (2006) Modern life leads to more depression among children, *The Daily Telegraph*: letter printed 12 September. Online. Available HTTP: <http://www.telegraph.co.uk/news/1528639/Modern-life-leads-to-more-depression-among-children.html> (Accessed 1 March 2011).

Alexander, R.J. (2004) *Towards Dialogic Teaching. Rethinking Classroom Talk*, York: Dialogos.

——(2008) The primary review. Emerging perspectives on childhood, speech delivered at the General Teaching Council for England conference, in conjunction with the Children's Society Good Childhood Inquiry and the Primary Review: *Childhood, Wellbeing and Education*, Westminster, 17 March 2008. Online. Available HTTP: <http://www.primaryreview.org.uk/Downloads/Childhood–Well-being_and_Primary_Education_Robin_Alexander_lecture_170308.pdf> (Accessed 01 March 2011).

Alexander, R.J. and Flutter, J. (2009) *Towards a New Primary Curriculum: A Report From the Cambridge Primary Review: Past and Present*. Cambridge: University of Cambridge Faculty of Education.

Anderson, T. (2004) Towards a theory of online learning, in T. Anderson and F. Elloumi (eds) *Theory and Practice of Online Learning*, Athabasca: Athabasca University.

Anderson, T. and Elloumi, F. (eds) (2004) *Theory and Practice of Online Learning*, Athabasca: Athabasca University.

Andrews, R. (ed.) (2004) *The Impact of ICT on Literacy Education*, London: RoutledgeFalmer.

Austin, R. and Anderson, J. (2008) *e-Schooling. Global messages from a Small Island*, Abingdon : David Fulton.

Bakhtin, M.M. [written during the 1930s] (1981) *The Dialogic Imagination: Four Essays*, Michael Holquist (ed.) Caryl Emerson and Michael Holquist (trans.), Austin, TX: University of Texas Press.

BECTA (2004*)* A review of the research literature on barriers to the uptake of ICT by teachers. Online. Available HTTP: <http://partners.BECTA.org.uk/page_documents/research/barriers.pdf> (Accessed 1 March 2011).

——(2008) Personalising learning in a connected world: a guide for school leaders. Online. Available HTTP: <http://publications.becta.org.uk/display.cfm?resID=35296> (Accessed 1 March 2011).

——(2008b) How to encourage pupils' creativity using ICT. Online. Available HTTP: <http://schools.becta.org.uk/index.php?section=tl&catcode=ss_tl_use_02& rid=594> (Accessed 1 March 2011).

——(2009) BECTA's contribution to the Rose review. Online. Available HTTP: <http://publications.becta.org.uk/display.cfm?resID=40240> (Accessed 1 March 2011).

Bennett, R., Hamill, A. and Pickford, T. (2007) *Progression in Primary ICT*, Abingdon: David Fulton Publishers Ltd.

Bennet, S., Maton, K. and Kervin, L. (2008) The 'digital natives': a critical review of the evidence, *British Journal of Educational Technology*, 39 (5), 775–86.

Bennett, R. and McBurnie, W. (2005) ICT and music-embedding ICT when teaching music and promoting creativity, in S. Wheeler (ed.) *Transforming Primary ICT*, Exeter: Learning Matters.

Bernstein, B. (2000) *Pedagogy, Symbolic Control and Identity: Theory, Research and Critique*, (revised edition), Oxford: Rowman and Littlefield.

Blogpulse (2011) Blogpulse stats, Nielsen. Online. Available HTTP: <http://www.blogpulse.com/> (Accessed 1 March 2011).

Bolduc, D. and Gonzalez, S. (2010) NH focus on ePortfolio Day, podcast of proceedings. Online. Available HTTP: <http://plymouth.edu/online/events/nhfocus_2010.html> (Accessed 1 March 2011).

British Education Suppliers Association (June 2009) ICT provision and use 2009/10. Online. Available HTTP: <http://resources.eun.org/insight/BESA_ICT2009_Summary.pdf> (Accessed 1 March 2011).

Buckingham, D. (2007) *Beyond Technology: Children's Learning in the Age of Digital Culture*, Cambridge: Polity Press.

Byron, T. (2008) Safer children in a digital world: the report of the Byron Review. Online. Available HTTP: <http://www.education.gov.uk/ukccis/userfiles/file/FinalReportBookmarked.pdf> (Accessed 1 March 2011).

——(2010) *Do We Have Safer Children in a Digital World? A Review of Progress Since the 2008 Byron Review*, London: Department for Children, Schools and Families. Online. Available HTTP: <http://www.dcsf.gov.uk/byronreview/pdfs/dopercent20wepercent20havepercent20safer percent20childrenpercent20inpercent20apercent20digitalpercent20world-WEB.pdf> (Accessed 1 March 2011).

Carrington, V. (2009) From Wikipedia to the humble classroom wiki, in V. Carrington and M. Robinson (eds) *Digital Literacies, Social Learning and Classroom Practices*. London: Sage.

Claire, H. and Woolley, R. (2007) What has creativity got to do with citizenship education?, in A. Wilson (ed.) *Creativity in Primary Education*, Exeter: Learning Matters.

Cohen, T (25 March 2009) Exit Winston Churchill, enter Twitter. The Mail Online. Available HTTP: <http://www.dailymail.co.uk/news/article-1164682/Exit-Winston-Churchill-enter-Twitter–Yes-new-primary-school-curriculum.html> (Accessed 1 March 2011).

Cole, G. (2007) Why every school should be podcasting, *Guardian,* 18 September. Online. Available HTTP: <http://www.guardian.co.uk/education/2007/sep/18/link.link16> (Accessed 14 March 2011)

Condie, R., Munro, B., Seagreaves, L. and Kenesson, S. (2007) The impact of ICT in schools – a landscape review. Online. Available HTTP: <http://publications.becta.org.uk/display.cfm?resID=28221& page=1835> (Accessed 1 March 2011).

Cornwall, J. (2008) Is technology ruining children? *Sunday Times*, 27 April 2008. Online. Available HTTP: <http://women.timesonline.co.uk/tol/life_and_style/women/families/article3805196.ece> (Accessed 1 March 2011).

Cox, M., Preston, C. and Cox, K. (2000) What factors support or prevent teachers from using ICT in their classroom?, Paper presented at the British Educational Research Association Annual Conference, University of Sussex at Brighton, 2–5 September 1999. Online. Available HTTP: <http://www.leeds.ac.uk/educol/documents/00001304.htm> (Accessed 1 March 2011).

Craig, O. (2009) Why a Twitter curriculum will only do our generation harm, *The Telegraph Online*, 4 April 2009. Online. Available HTTP: <http://www.telegraph.co.uk/comment/5106466/Baroness-Greenfield-why-a-Twittericulum-will-only-do-our-children-harm.html> (Accessed 1 March 2011).

Daniels, H. (2001) *Vygotsky and Pedagogy*, New York: Routledge.

Davies, J. and Merchant, G. (2009) Negotiating the blogosphere, in V. Carrington and M. Robinson (eds) *Digital Literacies, Social Learning and Classroom Practices*, London: Sage.

Department for Children, Schools and Families (2008a) *Practice Guidance for the Early Years Foundation Stage: Setting the Standards for Learning, Development and Care for Children from Birth to Five*, London: DCSF.

——(2008b) Personalised learning – a practical guide. Online. Available HTTP: <http://publica tions.teachernet.gov.uk/default.aspx?PageFunction=productdetails&PageMode=publications& ProductId=DCSF-00844-2008> (Accessed 1 March 2011).

DfE (2010) *The National Strategies*. Online. Available HTTP: <http://nationalstrategies.standards. dcsf.gov.uk/> (Accessed 1 March 2011).

DCSF (2009) The independent review of the primary curriculum: final report. Online. Available at HTTP: <http://www.education.gov.uk/publications/eOrderingDownload/Primary_curriculum_ Report.pdf> (Accessed 1 April 2011).

DFE (2011) The primary national strategies. Online. Available at HTTP: <http://nationalstrategies. standards.dcsf.gov.uk/primary.>. (Accessed 1 April 2011).

DFEE and QCA (1999) *The National Curriculum*. London: Crown Copyright and QCA.

Department for Education and Skills (2003) *Every Child Matters*. London: The Stationery Office.

——(2003b) Excellence and enjoyment: a strategy for primary schools. Online. Available HTTP: <http://nationalstrategies.standards.dcsf.gov.uk/node/85063> (Accessed 1 March 2011).

——(2004) *Pedagogy and Practice. Creating Effective Learners: Using ICT to Enhance Learning*. London: DfES.

Downes, S. (2005) E-learning 2.0, *eLearn Magazine*, 17 October. Online. Available HTTP: <http://www.elearnmag.org/subpage.cfm?section=articles&article=29–1> (Accessed 1 March 2011).

Etchingham, J. (2011) Are we putting our kids under too much pressure? *The Daily Telegraph,* 2 January Online. Available HTTP: <http://www.telegraph.co.uk/comment/8235111/Are-we-putting our-kids-under-too-much-pressure.html> (Accessed 1 April 2011).

Facer, K. and Williamson, B. (2004) Designing technologies to support creativity and collaboration: a handbook from Futurelab. Online. Available HTTP: <http://www.futurelab. org.uk/resources/documents/handbooks/creativity_and_collaboration.pdf> (Accessed 1 March 2011).

Feynman, R. (1999) *The Pleasure of Finding Thing Out*, London: Penguin.

Fisch, K. and McLeod, S. (2007) Did you know shift happens? Available HTTP: <http://shifth appens.wikispaces.com/Copyright> (Accessed 1 April 2011).

Frechette, J. (2002) *Developing Media Literacy in Cyberspace: Pedagogy and Critical Learning for the Twenty-First-Century Classroom*, Westport, CT: Praeger Publishers.

FutureLab (2007) The future of personalisation, *e-Learning Today*, 03, Spring 2007, 19–20.

Garner, R. (2011) Blog early. Blog often: the secret to making boys write. *The Independent*. Online. Available HTTP: <http://independent. co.uk/news/education/education-news/blog-early- blog-often-the-secret-to-making-boys-write-properly-2211232.html.

Garner, R. and Gillingham, M.G. (1996) *Internet Communications in Six Classrooms: Conversations Across Time, Space, and Culture*, Mahwah, NJ: Lawrence Erlbaum.

Gokhale, A. (1995) Collaborative learning enhances critical thinking, *Journal of Technology Education,* 7 (1), 22–30.

Green, H., Facer, K., Rudd, T., Dillon, P. and Humphreys, P. (2005) Personalised learning and digital technologies. Online. Available HTTP: <http://www.futurelab.org.uk/resources/publications reports-articles/opening-education-reports/Opening-Education-Report201/> (Accessed 1 March 2011).

Greenfield, S. (2008) *The Quest for Identity in the 21st Century*, London: Sceptre.

——(2009) How Facebook addiction is damaging your child's brain: a leading neuroscientist's chilling warning, *Daily Mail*, 23 April. Online. Available HTTP: <http://www.dailymail.co.uk/ femail/article-1172690/How-Facebook-addiction-damaging-childs-brain-A-leading-neuroscientists- chilling-warning.html#ixzz1EElvchIh> (Accessed 1 March 2011).

Halsey, S. (2007) Embracing emergent technologies and envisioning new ways of using them for literacy learning in the primary classroom, *English Teaching:Practice and Critique,* 6 (2). Online. Available HTTP: <http://education.waikato.ac.nz/research/files/etpc/2007v6n2nar2. pdf> (Accessed 14 March 2011).

Hamersley, B. (2004) Audible revolution, *The Guardian Online.* Online. Available HTTP: http://www.guardian.co.uk/media/2004/feb/12/broadcasting.digitalmedia (Accessed 1 March 2011).

Hargreaves, D. (2005) About learning: report of the learning working group. Online. Available, HTTP: <http://www.demos.co.uk//publications//aboutlearning> (Accessed 1 March 2011).

——(2006) A new shape for schooling, specialist schools and academies trust. Online. Available HTTP: <http://www.ssat-inet.net/en-gb/PDF/A%20new%20shape%20for%20schooling%20-% 20Chpaters%201%20and%202.pdf> (Accessed 1 March 2010).

Howe, W. (2010) An anecdotal history of the people and communities that brought about the internet and the web. Online. Available HTTP: <http://www.walthowe.com/navnet/history. html> (Accessed 1 March 2011).

Jaffer, S. (2009) Educational technology pedagogy: a looseness of fit between learning theories and pedagogy, *Education as Change,* 14(2): 273–87.

Kennewell, S. (2006) Reflections on the interactive whiteboard phenomenon, a synthesis of research from the UK, paper presented at the AARE Conference, Adelaide, November 2006. Online. Available HTTP: <http://www.aare.edu.au/06pap/ken06138.pdf> (Accessed 1 March 2011).

Kennewell, S., Parkinson, J. and Tanner, H. (2000) *Developing the ICT Capable School,* London: Routledge.

Kress, G. and van Leeuwen, T. (2000) *Multimodal Discourse,* London: Arnold.

Lankshear, C. and Knoble, M. (2008) *Digital Literacies. Concepts, Policies and Practices.* Oxford: Peter Lang.

Lees, J. (2009) e-make overs, *e-Learning Today,* 07, Spring 2009, 56–7.

Livingstone, S. (2008) Taking risky opportunities in youthful content creation: teenagers' use of social networking sites for intimacy, privacy and self-expression, *New Media and Society,* 10 (3) 393–411.

Loveless, A. (2002) Literature review in creativity, new technologies and learning. Online. Available HTTP: <http://www.futurelab.org.uk/resources/documents/lit_reviews/Creativity_Review. pdf> (Accessed 1 March 2011).

McLeod, J. and Vasinda, S. (2009) Web2.0 affordance for literacies, in T. Kidd and I. Chen, (eds) *An Educator's Guide to Web 2.0.* Charlotte, NC: Information Age Publishing Inc, pp. 233–45.

McCluhan, M. (1964) *Understanding Media: The Extensions of Man,* New York: McGraw Hill.

Merchant, G. (2007) Daleks and other avatars: virtual lives in real classrooms, Draft paper. Online. Available HTTP: <http://extra.shu.ac.uk/bvw/virtual%20world%20paper.doc> (Accessed 1 March 2011).

Miliband, D. (2004) Personalised learning: building a new relationship with schools, speech by David Miliband, 8 January 2004, North of England Education Conference, Belfast. Online. Available HTTP: <http://publications.education.gov.uk/eOrderingDownload/personalised-learning.pdf> (Accessed 1 March 2010).

Montessori, Maria (1917) *The Advanced Montessori Method: Spontaneous Activity in Education,* Vol. 1 (trans. Florence Simmonds (1965)), Cambridge: Robert Bentley.

Moore, M.G. (1991) Distance education theory, *The American Journal of Distance Education,* 5(3). Online. Available HTTP: <http://www.ajde.com/Contents/vol5_3.htm>.

National Advisory Committee on Creative and Cultural Education (1999) All our futures: creativity, culture and education. Online. Available HTTP: <http://www.cypni.org.uk/downloads/ allourfutures.pdf> (Accessed 1 March 2011).

Naughton, J. (1999) *A Brief History of The Future: The Origins of the Internet,* London: Weidenfeld and Nicolson.

NHDE (New Hampshire Department of Education) (2005) NH code of administrative rules-education, Part Ed 306 Minimum Standards For Public School Approval, 306.42. Online. Available HTTP: <http://www.education.nh.gov/legislation/documents/ed306.pdf> (Accessed, 1 March 2011).

O'Brien, C. (2008) How the Google generation thinks differently, *The Times Online*, 9 July 2008. Online. Available HTTP: <http://women.timesonline.co.uk/tol/life_and_style/women/families/article4295414.ece> (Accessed 1 March 2011).

OFSTED (2008) Geography in school: changing practice. Online. Available HTTP: <http://www.ofsted.gov.uk/Ofsted-home/Publications-and-research/Browse-all-by/Education/Curriculum/Geography/Primary/Geography-in-schools-changing-practice/(language)/eng-GB> (Accessed 23 March 2011).

——(2010) The safe use of new technologies. Online. Available HTTP: <http://www.ofsted.gov.uk/Ofsted-home/Publications-and-research/Browse-all-by/Documents-by-type/Thematic-reports/The-safe-use-of-new-technologies> (Accessed 1 March 2011).

O'Reilly, T. (2005) What is Web 2.0? *O'Reilly Network*. Online. Available HTTP: <http://www.oreillynet.com/pub/a/oreilly/tim/news/2005/09/30/what-is-web-20.html> (Accessed 7 February 2011).

ORCSD (Oyster River Cooperative School District) (2010) K-12 Digital portfolios. Online. Available HTTP: <http://www.orcsd.org/index.php?option=com_content&view=article&id=107&Itemid=138> (Accessed 1 March 2011).

Palmer, S. (2006) *Toxic Childhood: How the Modern World is Damaging Our Children and What We Can Do about It*, London: Orion.

——(2008) *Detoxing Childhood. What Parents Need to Know to Raise Bright, Balanced Children*, London: Orion.

Papert, S. (1980) *Mindstorms: Children, Computers, and Powerful Ideas*, London: Basic Books.

——(1993) *The Children's Machine: Rethinking School in the Age of the Computer*. London: Harvester Wheatsheaf.

Parker, J. Palmer (1998) *The Courage to Teach*, San Francisco, CA: Jossey-Bass.

Paton, G. (26 March 2009) Twitter is put on the new primary school curriculum. *The Telegraph Online*. Available HTTP: <http://www.telegraph.co.uk/technology/twitter/5050261/Twitter-is-put-on-new-primary-school-curriculum.html> (Accessed 1 March 2011).

Prensky, M. (2001) Digital natives. Digital immigrants. *On the Horizon*, 9 (5): Available HTTP: <http://www.twitchspeed.com> (Accessed 1 March 2011).

——(2003) Has 'Growing up digital' and extensive video game playing affected younger military personnel's skill sets? paper presented at I/ITSEC 2003. Online. Available HTTP: <http://www.marcprensky.com/writing/Prenskypercent20-percent20Haspercent20Growingpercent20Uppercent20Digitalpercent20Affectedpercent20Militarypercent20Skillpercent20Sets.pdf> (Accessed 1 March 2011).

Pritchard, A. (2007) *Effective Teaching with Internet Technologies*, London: Sage.

Puttnam, D. (2008) Building schools for the future, Futurelab podcast. Online. Available HTTP: <http://media.futurelab.org.uk/podcasts/becta_talks/lord_puttnam/> (Accessed 1 March 2011).

QCA (1998) *Schemes of Work for Key Stages 1 and 2*, London: QCA.

QCDA (2010) The National Curriculum online. Online. Available HTTP: <http://curriculum.qcda.gov.uk/key-stages-1-and-2/learning-across-the-curriculum/creativity/index.aspx>

Richardson, W. (2006) *Blogs, Wikis, Podcasts, and Other Powerful Web Tools for Classrooms*, Thousand Oaks, CA: Corwin Press.

Rose, J. (2009) The Independent Review of the Primary Curriculum. Online. Available HTTP: <http://publications.education.gov.uk/default.aspx?PageFunction=productdetails&PageMode=publications&ProductId=DCSF-00499-2009>

Rosenberg, S. (2009) *Say Everything: How Blogging Began, What It's Becoming, and Why It Matters*, second Edition, New York: Three Rivers Press.

Rosenzweig, R. (2006) Can history be open source? Wikipedia and the future of the past, *The Journal of American History*, 93(1), 117–46.

Seib, C. (2010) Is there such a thing as internet addiction? *The Times Online*, 10 March 2010. Online. Available HTTP: <http://women.timesonline.co.uk/tol/life_and_style/women/the_way_we_live/article7052999.ece> (Accessed 1 March 2011).

Selwyn, N. (2011) *Education and Technology: Key Issues and Debates*. New York: Continuum International Publishing Group.

Stacy, S. (2006) Know it all, can Wikipedia conquer expertise? Annals of Information, New York Times. Online. Available HTTP <http://www.newyorker.com/archive/2006/07/31/060731fa_fact> (Accessed 1 March 2011).

Steiner Waldorf Schools Fellowship (2010) FAQ: When is IT taught in Steiner schools? Online. Available HTTP: http://www.steinerwaldorf.org.uk/faqs.html#it. (Accessed 1 March 2011).

Teachernet (2004) What does personalised learning mean to you? Online. Available HTTP: <http://www.teachernet.gov.uk/teachers/issue31/primary/features/Whatdoespersonalisedlearningmeantoyou_Primary/> (Accessed 1 March 2011).

Teachers' TV (2008) Blogs and wikis. Teachers Television, 15 December. Online. Available HTTP: http://www.teachers.tv/videos/blogs-wikis. (Accessed 1 April 2011).

Teachers TV (2008) Journey Sticks, currently located at TES connect. Online. Available HTTP: <http://www.tes.co.uk/teaching-resource/teachers-tv-journey-sticks-6048401/> (Accessed 22 August 2011).

Teachers TV (2010) Primary Geography: Overseas localities, currently located at TES Connect. Online. Available HTTP <http://www.tes.co.uk/teaching-resource/teachers-tv-primary-geography-overseas-localities-6044215/> (Accessed 22 August 2011).

Torgerson, C.J. and Zhu, D. (2004) A systematic review and meta-analysis of the effectiveness of ICT on literacy learning in English, in R. Andrews (ed.), *The Impact of ICT on Literacy Education*, London: RoutledgeFalmer.

Underwood, J. (2009) Personalising learning, BECTA. Online. Available HTTP: <http://partners.becta.org.uk/page_documents/research/reports/personalised_learning.pdf> (Accessed 1 March 2011).

UNICEF (2007) Child poverty in perspective: an overview of child well-being in rich countries. Online. Available HTTP: <http://www.unicef-irc.org/publications/pdf/rc7_eng.pdf> (Accessed 1 March 2011).

Vygotsky, L.S. (1978) *Mind and Society: The Development of Higher Psychological Processes*, Cambridge, MA: Harvard University Press.

Ward Cunningham, H. and Leuf, B. (2005) *The Wiki Way: Quick Collaboration on the Web*, fifth edition, Reading, MA: Addison-Wesley.

Weller, M. (2007) *Virtual Learning Environments: Using, Choosing and Developing Your VLE*, London: Routledge.

Wenger, E. (2004) *Communities of Practice Learning, Meaning and Identity*, Cambridge: Cambridge University Press.

Wheeler, S. (ed.) (2005) *Transforming Primary ICT*, Exeter: Learning Matters.

Wild, M. (1996) Technology refusal: rationalising the failure of student and beginning teachers to use computers, *British Journal of Educational Technology*, 27 (2), 134–43.

Zakon, R. (2010) 'Hobbes' internet timeline 10.1. Online. Available HTTP: <http://www.zakon.org/robert/internet/timeline/> (Accessed 21 February 2011).

Ziegler, S. (2007) The (mis)education of generation M, *Learning, Media and Technology*, 32 (1), 70.

Index